WITHDRAWN

WHY WORRY WHEN GOD. . .

Table of Contents

Foreword ix
Preface. xiii

Chapter 1. An Introduction to Water

The Water Planet

Worldwide Water Circulation 1
Water and Living Organisms 3
Water Throughout History. 4

Water is Wealth

The Value of Water. 5
Water as a Biomaterial. 6
Water Conservation. 7

We Are Water Beings

The Ocean Within. 8
The Earth from Outer Space. 9

Chapter 2. The Pieces of the Water Puzzle

The Unusual Properties of Water

Boiling Point and Freezing Point. 13
Density. 14
Specific Heat. 14
Viscosity 15
Surface Tension 16
Memory. 16

Chapter 3. The Specific Structure of Water
The Hexagonal Key

H_2O -The Chemical Formula of Water

Covalent Bonding. 22
Hydrogen Bonding. 27
The Water Dance .29

Hexagonal Water - The Puzzle Solved
    Temperature 31
    The Puzzle of Molecular Weight. 33
    Specific Heat 34
    What is Super-cooled Water? 35
    Density 37
    Viscosity 39
    Water - The Ultimate Energy Carrier and
        Waste Removal System 39
    Water's Memory .40

Chapter 4. Water Structure at Interfaces
Water and Ions
    Structure-making vs. Structure-
        breaking ions 46
    The Hydration of Ions 49
Water Structure and Ions Within the Body
    Calcium Within the Body 52
    Electrolytes (ions) in Bodily Fluids. 54
Water and Proteins
    Layers of Water 56
    Blood Plasma. 58
    Hexagonal Water and DNA 58
    Water and Collagen 61
    Thermal Protection of Proteins. 62

Chapter 5. Hexagonal Water and Human Health
    The Molecular Water Environment Theory. . .67
    Methods of Producing Hexagonal Water . . .68
    Aging and the Molecular Water Environment. . .69
    Cell Water Turnover. 71
    Aging is a Loss of Structured Water 73
    The Issue of Weight. 73

Hexagonal Water Supports Metabolic
  Efficiency 74
The Water of Longevity 75
The Relationship between Survival and
  Hexagonal Water 76
Water, Calcium and Aging 78
Osteoporosis 80
Hexagonal Water Prevents Illness 81
Hexagonal Water Enhances the Immune
  System 83
Vitamin C and Hexagonal Water. 85
Diabetes and Cancer 86
A Strategy for Beating AIDS. 95
Water and Digestion. 97
Water Contamination and Health 99

Chapter 6. Drinking Hexagonal Water
Hexagonal Water for Health 103
Biological Organisms Prefer Hexagonal
  Water 104
Hexagonal Water - the Best Water
  to Drink! 106
Creating Hexagonal Water 107
Is Drinking Cold Water Better? 108
Beyond Theory. 108
Final Words. 109

Appendix - the use of NMR to verify molecular size . .115

About the Author 119

Author's Bibliography. .125

Foreword
by MJ Pangman
editor of the English translation

My first exposure to Dr. Mu Shik Jhon was while doing research on the subject of Hexagonal Water. I ran across a quote from his book and I remember trying to find the complete text. Unfortunately, at that time an English translation did not exist. If it had been available then, my education on the subject would have taken a lot less time and required a lot less effort.

When I was introduced to Hexagonal Water, there was very little written in terms that a lay person could understand. For the most part, this is still the case because an understanding of the molecular structure of water requires a knowledge of biochemistry, molecular and quantum biology and a whole list of analytical techniques including nuclear magnetic resonance, X-ray diffraction, various methods of spectroscopy, etc.

The structure of water is a complex subject and yet with a bit of background, and without getting too involved in the mathematical equations, it can be understood. **That is the beauty of this book!**

Dr. Jhon has taken years of research and condensed it into a simple treatise that will help you to understand why Hexagonal Water is an important key to your health. In fact, he has made it so simple that before you begin to read the book, I think you should be aware of a few of his accomplishments.

Dr. Mu Shik Jhon has published nearly 300 scientific papers. His *Significant Structure Theory of Water* was published early in his career in conjunction with the world famous scientist, Dr. Henry Eyring and his first book, Significant Liquid Structures (John Wiley & Sons -1969) is continually referenced in the academic world. Dr. Jhon has received dozens of awards and honors, including the Presidential award of Science (the highest scientific award in Korea). He is currently president of four scientific organizations and is director of the Molecular Science Research Center in Korea. He is Chairman of the Board of The Korean Academy of Science and Technology and his list of invited speaking engagements goes on and on. He is still an invited lecturer at many colleges and scientific gatherings. His brilliance is known in the world of science even if his name is unfamiliar outside the academic circle.

Lastly, let me say that I have been drinking Hexagonal Water for over 3 years. My personal experience with this vitalizing water has been noteworthy. Within 3 weeks of drinking several glasses of Hexagonal Water each day, I experienced deep tissue cleansing (known as a healing reaction). Since that time I have experienced fewer colds and more energy.

I have also participated in Bio Impedance testing (tests which can measure the intracellular and extracellular water movement within the body). Hexagonal Water unquestionably enhances cell water turn-over, taking nutrients in and expelling wastes with greater ease than bottled waters. I have experienced the difference and now it is the only water I drink!

Enjoy this book – the first of its kind to explain water structure in simple terms: The Water Puzzle and the Hexagonal Key.

Preface

I am considered an expert in the field of statistical liquid mechanics. From the very beginning, my work challenged traditional thinking and it has resulted in a flurry of research on the subject of water structure. Within the pages of this book, the reader will find information on hexagonally-structured water, which according to my research is the *water of life*.

After more than 40 years of research, it is obvious to me that our awareness of water is still in the "passive" phase. Although we depend on this precious resource for our lives, we have not understood its mysteries enough to take "active" steps to preserve its quality. However, scholars and medical experts in many nations are finally paying attention to the fact that our health can be improved by improving the quality of our water and that illnesses can actually be *treated* with water.

This realization is causing more emphasis to be placed on environmental issues and many nations are beginning to take action. Because I lecture in many parts of the world, I can confirm that an awareness of the connection between water and health is growing and as a scholar who has devoted his life to spreading this awareness, I feel a deep sense of gratification.

On the other hand, there is still a great lack of understanding regarding the relationship of water to our health. In most cases we tend to oversimplify the usefulness of water, placing blind faith in any source. But all water is not created equal and it is the *structure* of the water within our bodies that ultimately determines health or sickness.

Magnetic Resonance Imaging (MRI) is a useful tool for measuring water structure within the human body. It can help to discern normal and abnormal tissues, based on the structure of the water within. Accordingly, the structure of the water within the body can now be used to determine whether or not an individual is afflicted with disease.

Although the subject of water structure can be very complex, I have tried to make this book easy to read - to use simple terms and to provide basic information in a language that is easily understood. It is my hope that it will increase awareness and ultimately affect the water we choose to drink as well as the ways we choose to safeguard the earth's limited supply.

Dr. Mu Shik Jhon

THE
WATER PUZZLE

An Introduction to Water

Chapter

1

Chapter 1
An Introduction to Water

The Water Planet

Water is a dynamic medium, continually changing from liquid, to solid, to gas. As it cycles from its gaseous phase in the atmosphere, to its liquid and solid forms on the earth, it provides life for an entire planet. Yet, as important as water is to our survival, our scientific minds have not been able to determine its origin or its true essence. To this day, water remains one of life's puzzles.

Worldwide Water Circulation

The total amount of water on the earth and in the atmosphere has been calculated to be between 1.3 and 1.4 billion km^3. That total volume never changes – it merely recycles. Three quarters of the surface of the earth is covered by oceans, comprising 97.2% of the total water volume on earth. 2.15% is in the form of ice and .001% is included in the atmosphere which surrounds the earth. Of all the water that continually cycles and recycles on the earth's surface, only a small percentage is actually available for our use. Usable water includes underground aquifers and above-ground rivers, lakes, streams, and marshes, comprising only .65% of the total water on the planet. The earth, the third planet from the sun, contains one hundred forty-six ten thousand trillion tons of water – an amount that is difficult to imagine. Surely the earth is worthy of its name – the water planet!

At this very moment, water is involved in a continuous cycle. It evaporates from the oceans and moves through the atmosphere, traveling on wind currents. As the cycle continues, vapor in the atmosphere ultimately changes form and falls to the earth as rain or snow – ending up in rivers and oceans to begin the cycle all over again. Along the way, water nourishes the land and all forms of life on the planet. This cycle continues every day just like any typical summer event, endowing the inhabitants of earth with enormous benefits – and occasional calamities.

On a smaller scale, but in a similar manner, water circulates through all living organisms. It is absorbed from the soil by plants and is consumed by higher life forms to follow a circulatory course through all living organisms. The amount of water that goes into any organism is the same amount that is expelled and the cycle does not stop as long as the organism is alive and healthy.

Water and Living Organisms

The earliest philosophers recognized that water was the source of life. The Greek philosopher, Thales (6th century B.C.) identified water as the "foundational structure of the universe" and Asian philosophy defined water as the "beginning and the basis of all creation." Water circulation helps maintain balance on the earth and within biological organisms. In the living organism, water delivers nutrients and oxygen and discharges metabolic wastes. When water is lacking, even slightly, all types of illness can result.

Human beings can survive for many days without food, but when they cannot drink water for even three or four days, they suffer dire consequences. 60 to 70% of the adult human body is water. 90% of blood is water and 75% of muscle tissue is water. In order to live, human beings must drink between one to three liters of water every day. As for water inside the human body; ideally, 60% is found inside the cells (intracellular), and the remaining 40% is situated outside the cells (extracellular). Of the extracellular water, 10% is found in the blood.

In nature, water movement is an indicator of energy and purity. Water that is moving is generally better than the stagnant water found in reservoirs or from public water sources. Turbulent water contains considerable oxygen and minerals and it is highly energized. Typically, when movement is created, water becomes a source of living energy.

> **In nature, water movement is an indicator**
> **of energy and purity.**
> **Turbulent water contains considerable oxygen**
> **and minerals and it is highly energized.**

Water Throughout History

Water is the source that cultivates life and sustains it. According to the United Nations, about 25,000 die every day from water-related illnesses. It is also reported that if clean water were available everywhere, the child mortality rate would be decreased by 90%. Historically, only those civilizations that could control their supply of water were successful. Accordingly, all the major civilizations throughout history have begun around large rivers. For example:

- The Mesopotamian civilization at the river valley of the Tigres and Euphrates Rivers
- The Chinese civilization on the Huang Ho River
- The Indian civilization along the Ganges River
- The Egyptian civilization on the Nile

The major civilizations which developed along large rivers differ from smaller cultures in mountainous or arid regions. These smaller cultures had to depend on their resourcefulness, which resulted in the development of innovative methods to manage their water supply.

4

There is evidence that Arab cultures used wells as early as 3,000 B.C., while irrigation practices developed in the mountainous regions. In my own country of Korea, the rainfall gauge was invented in 1448 AD. It is recognized as the world's first rainfall measurement device.

The organized study of water began in ancient Greece where it was long considered a philosophical science and referred to as *hydrography*. Only recently (within the last 100 years) has the study of water taken on a science of its own and the term "hydrology" has been coined. Today, the study of water is thriving – linking water to life, health and the prevention of disease.

Water is Wealth

The Value of Water

The paper in this book contains more water than you can imagine. Without it, you would not be able to turn the pages without shattering them. Moisture in the air helps you to breathe and keeps the membranes of your nose and throat from drying out. There is no other material that is so close to us, yet since water exists everywhere, we tend to forget its value.

The relationship between water and civilization is also so close that we forget its importance. Any nation that fails to generate cost-effective, clean water is considered an underdeveloped nation. For this reason, most countries in the world consider water as wealth. When water is utilized effectively, it can transform deserts into fertile land and can generate an infinite number of benefits. In other words, water can be used for drinking, agriculture, commerce, power generation, transportation, cleansing, leisure, tourism etc. It has the potential to solve food and energy-related problems as well as to contribute in many other ways.

Water as a Biomaterial

Theoretically, it is possible to transform water in the liquid state into solid matter, comparable to plastic, by transforming the bonded multi-dimensional molecular form into a flat surface. Experiments are now underway to use water in this way as a raw material in the creation of construction materials – even thread for clothing. This research began in Russia and is gaining momentum. The theory is based, in part, on the response of water under pressure and magnetic fields inside capillary tubes. Under these circumstances it becomes well ordered and assumes a flat surface-type structure. This structure has properties like a gel – somewhere between the liquid and solid states and it is bonded so tightly that it does not boil at 100° C. – nor does it freeze, even at -40° C.

It is not an overstatement to say that we are headed for an amazing revolution where water is concerned. The era in which people reside in homes and wear clothes made of water, may not be far off.

> **It is not an overstatement to say that
> we are headed for an amazing revolution
> where water is concerned.**

Water Conservation

Unfortunately the amount of water on the planet is limited. The amount does not change. However, the number of people who require water increases every day. And that is not all. Changes in our lifestyle have led to significant increases in the amount of water needed for each person. The fact that the amount of water does not change, yet population increases, poses potential problems for the survival of our species. Although it is said that the water resources of the world are still sufficient, many countries are facing water shortages.

Because of water shortages in various locations, we are beginning to develop methods of purifying salt water from the oceans and of obtaining it from the air. The era in which water was available for free no longer exists. Water is now an economic product – a source of wealth.

We are Water Beings

You are a lump of water! And that "lump of water" which is your body is involved in thousands of bodily functions. The saliva you use to begin diges-

7

tion and to swallow, is mostly water. Your view of the horizon is made possible because your eyes move freely in a lubricant that is mostly water. The movement of your muscles is only possible because they are mostly water and because they receive their instructions via nerve impulses which are transmitted in water. Within living systems, everything happens in water.

The Ocean Within

It is a well-known fact that human blood closely resembles the chemistry of the ocean. (see Table 1) In other words, the human body is like the earth and it carries an ocean within it. From a scientific point of view, this is not an accident and it supports the theory that all life began in the ocean.

The oceans are not only the mother of life, they also play an important role in stabilizing the climate. Land that is closer to the ocean is subject to more frequent shifts in weather, however, water acts as an environmental shock-absorber. This is the reason for milder climates along the coastal regions. Heat from

Table 1. Composition of Ocean Water & Human Blood

Electrolyte	Chloride ion	Sulfide ion	Sodium ion	Potassium ion	Calcium ion	Magnesium ion
Ocean Water	55.2	7.7	30.6	1.1	1.2	3.7
Blood*	40.1	10.9	34.8	1.9	2.1	4.8

*averaged weight (%)

the sun is absorbed by the water and temperature changes are confined to a narrower range.

The Earth From Outer Space

Suppose that the planet earth were to be observed from outer space. Observers might record:

"Surprisingly, 70% of the third planet in this solar system is covered with liquid of a very flexible make-up with a simple molecular structure. The beings of this planet use the term 'water' for this substance and they too are 'water beings,' composed of 70% water - just like the planet. Though the 'water beings' are largely composed of water, they do not appear to realize its value. The water on the planet is treated negligently and wasted. It appears that the 'water beings' do not yet understand the essence of their being or the source of their origin."

Truly, we know very little about the essence of our being. I consider my knowledge to be merely the tip of the iceberg but one thing I do know... Water is the source of our lives and it is directly connected with our health. Paying attention to the kind of water we drink can have a greater influence on our health than any other one thing!

**Water is the source of our lives
and it is directly connected
with our health.**

THE
WATER PUZZLE

The Pieces of the Water Puzzle

Chapter
2

THE WATER PUZZLE

Chapter 2
The Pieces of the Water Puzzle

The story of my connection to water might be considered a "romance." Like most scientists, I am a dreamer. For over 40 years I have researched and experimented – driven by the desire to see the unseen and to understand the mysteries of the universe. Water is one of the mysteries to which I am especially drawn.

The Unusual Properties of Water

Boiling Point and Freezing Point

Water is indeed a puzzle with many properties that defy explanation. For example: Most students know that water freezes at 0° C and boils at 100° C, however if water were to follow the pattern of the other liquids in its class, it would boil at -60° C and freeze at -90° C – a huge discrepancy.

Water belongs to a class of compounds called hydrides in the oxygen family. The melting point and specific heat are calculated according to the molecular weight of each compound. Accordingly, water should be a vapor at normal living temperatures and if water were to follow the pattern determined by other liquids in the same class, there would be very little (if any) liquid water on the planet.

Density

One of the things my early research helped to clarify, was the reason for water's unusual density. Most substances contract (increase in density) as the temperature falls. Water is different. Its density reaches a maximum at 4° C. just above freezing. After that, it begins to expand as it freezes. Although this is highly unusual, it is the reason that ice floats rather than sinking to the bottom of a body of water. It is also the reason that lakes do not freeze from the bottom up and it is the reason that icebergs do not build up on the bottom of the ocean. Water's unusual changes in density were some of our first indicators that water had a unique structure. This property holds many keys relative to health, which will be explored later.

Specific Heat

The thermal properties of water are also very unique when compared to other liquids. Water has an unusually large heat capacity (the largest known), allowing it to absorb a considerable amount of heat with a minimal change in temperature. This is of great significance for biological organisms. It means that the human body can resist temperature changes even when environmental temperatures are extreme.

When water freezes, it releases a considerable amount of heat. When it vaporizes, it absorbs heat. The heat of fusion reaches 80cal/g. and the heat of vaporization reaches 540cal/g. - both of which are unusually high when compared to other liquids.

Since the specific heat (the amount of heat required to raise the temperature of a substance by 1 degree) of water is so high, climatic changes near the oceans are not nearly so extreme. Temperature changes from day to night are minimal along the coast compared to day and night fluctuations in the desert where there is little water.

Viscosity

Most liquids become more viscous (sticky, thick, resistant to flow) when pressure is exerted on them. Here again, water is quite different. In the case of water, viscosity decreases (rather than increases) as pressure is exerted at temperatures under 30° C. This phenomenon is another indicator that water structure is changing as the pressure varies.

Surface Tension

The reason that water droplets form beads rather than spreading out evenly over a surface is because water molecules form relatively strong hydrogen bonds (see chapter 3). What this means is that water molecules have a stronger attraction for each other than for other substances. This creates what is known as a high degree of surface tension and allows water to rise easily in small areas (capillaries). It accounts for the enhanced ability of water to move inside plants, within the soil matrix and into the interstitial spaces of the body. Other than mercury, water has the highest surface tension of any liquid.

Memory

An intriguing quality about water, and one that has only recently begun to be explored, is that it has the ability to "remember." Water will hold the frequency or vibration of a substance which has been placed in it – even after the substance has been removed. In other words, there is a lasting effect when water is influenced with any form of energy and it has the ability to carry this energy for prolonged periods of time. This property has significant implications in the field of health and healing.

There are dozens of "abnormalities" surrounding the properties of water. One thing is quite certain - water could not exhibit so many unusual character-istics unless it had unique structural qualities. In fact, this is the case. The abnormalities of water are our best clue to understanding its unique structure as we shall see in the next chapter.

> The abnormalities of water
> are our best clue to understanding
> its
> unique structure.

THE WATER PUZZLE

THE
WATER PUZZLE

The Specific Structure of Water

Chapter

3

Chapter 3
The Specific Structure of Water
The Hexagonal Key

Up to this point, we have examined the value of water and its unusual properties. In this chapter we will explore the *Specific Structure of Water.* We will show how the pieces of the *Water Puzzle* begin to come together once we understand *The Hexagonal Key.* This chapter is a bit tedious but I promise to keep it simple.

H_2O - the Chemical Formula of Water

H_2O is the formula for water - two hydrogen atoms joined with one oxygen atom. However, if it were as simple as that, water could not exhibit the unusual properties it is known for. **Water is not merely a collection of individual H_2O molecules.** Instead, water in the liquid state is characterized by a specific structure, $(H_2O)n$, where "n" equals the number of H_2O molecules that are joined together.

How are these water molecules joined? And, what is the nature of their structure? To understand this, we need a bit of basic chemistry.

Covalent Bonding

All the atoms that exist in the world are made up of a nucleus and electrons. Electrons are like a cloud that surrounds the nucleus. Within this cloud are layers or shells of electrons. The first electron shell contains one orbit which can accommodate up to two electrons. When the shell is complete, it is stable and less likely to react.

The second electron shell can contain up to 8 electrons – with 4 different orbits of 2 electrons each. Like the first shell, it is most stable when it is complete – in this case with 8 electrons.

The hydrogen atom, being the first element on the periodic table, contains only 1 electron. This leaves one vacancy in its first and only electron shell. Since Hydrogen is more stable with a complete electron shell (2 electrons), it seeks stability by sharing electrons. In this way, both are stable and the atoms are said to be *covalently bonded*. In nature, Hydrogen exists as H_2 where 2 Hydrogen atoms share electrons.

Figure 1 shows the state in which two Hydrogen atoms are covalently bonded. With this arrangement, hydrogen can be stable and less vulnerable to external influences. It has been noted that this type of bonding is similar to the stability offered in a marriage, where two individuals support each other and are not as likely to get involved with other partners as long as the marriage is satisfactory.

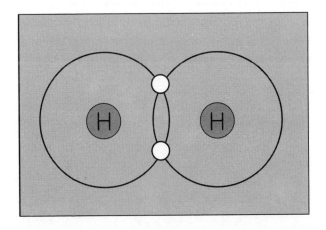

Fig. 1 Hydrogen (H₂) Covalent Bonding

The oxygen atom contains 8 electrons. With two electrons in the first shell, this leaves 6 electrons which are dispersed in the 4 available orbits of the outer shell. Oxygen has 2 vacancies to fill.

Figure 2 is a representation of the simple water molecule, showing the stabilization of both Hydrogen and Oxygen by the sharing of electrons.

Orbits with established electron paths are like *firmly grasped hands* – they do not easily engage in combinations. On the other hand (no pun intended), vacancies in electron orbits are like *open hands* reaching out for stability (see Figure 3). In the case of Hydrogen and Oxygen, a covalent bond is the answer and both atoms gain stability via the sharing of electrons. In this case, the covalent bond, completely changes the nature of the individual substances and a new compound is formed. Both hydrogen and oxygen are gases at normal temperatures, but when electrons are shared in this type of bonding, the result is a liquid – water.

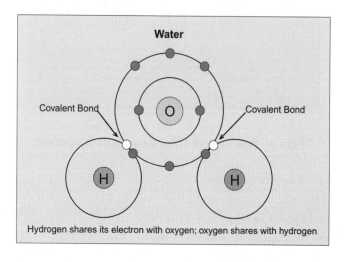

Fig. 2 The Simple Water Molecule

Figure 3 shows the Oxygen atom from a 3-dimensional perspective, with two vacancies (open hands) in two different orbital directions of the outer electron shell.

Typically, "hands" that are firmly grasped do not form chemical bonds, but this does not mean it is not possible. If these firmly grasped hands can be opened, they become useful in chemical combinations.

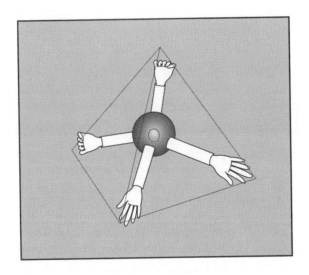

Fig. 3 The 3-Dimensional Oxygen Atom

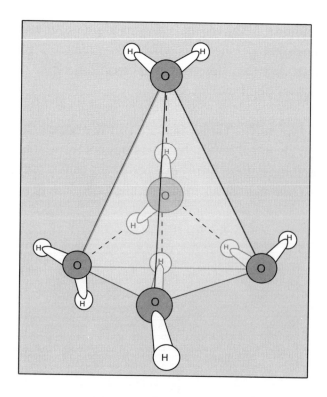

Fig. 4 The Water Tetrahedron

Figure 4 is the blueprint of the H_2O molecule. As shown, H_2O exists in the form of a tetrahedron, comprised of four regular triangles. Although the tetrahedron is slightly distorted in the actual water molecule, we can consider it a regular tetrahedron for our purposes, here.

As you can see, Oxygen forms the center of the tetrahedron and the Hydrogen atoms connect with ad-joining Oxygen atoms at the corners. The double lines connecting Oxygen and Hydrogen atoms represent covalent bonds. Dotted lines show another type of bond, called a hydrogen bond, which joins individual water molecules together - explained below.

Hydrogen Bonding

Hydrogen bonds are weaker bonds than covalent bonds. They result as an attraction between positive and negative charges.

Because of the direction that the Hydrogen and Oxygen "hands" reach out to join each other, water is a *polar* substance. It has a positively-charged side and a negatively-charged side (See Figure 5).

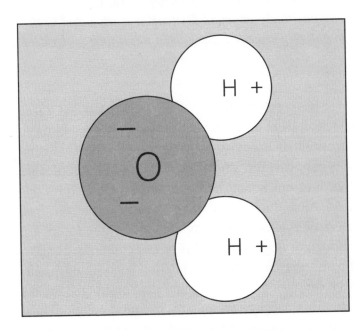

Fig. 5 The Water Dipole

These charges attract one another to form *Hydrogen bonds* (Figure 6) which hold water molecules together and give water a fluid characteristic.

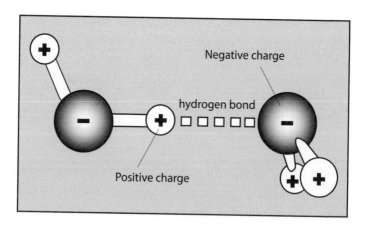

Fig. 6 The Hydrogen Bond
The positively-charged Hydrogen is attracted to the negatively-charged Oxygen in adjoining molecules of water.

The question arises, "What happens when a free electron from an adjoining molecule moves through the orbit of an existing molecule?" The first time this happens, it disturbs the stability of the molecule but does not break the bond - like a flirtatious confrontation during marriage. However, if the free electron passes through again, the reactive forces are enough to negate the stability and cause the bond to break - the partners are separated because of the intervention of a third party and the "marriage" breaks up. This happens frequently in liquid water. Thus, water is a continually changing medium.

The Water Dance

In the world of water, there is no place for the loner - single molecules do not last long in a fast-paced dance where small groupings predominate. The single H_2O molecule is a rare occurrence and is quickly snapped up by new partners that change every 100 billionths of a second. Water molecules join hands to form small groups, which gather and separate so quickly that visual confirmation has thus far been impossible. Computer simulation and X-ray diffraction have been the best methods for verifying the nature of this water dance.

Water molecules find stability by joining hands in groups of varying sizes – the most natural and stable of which are groupings of 5 and 6 (pentagonal and hexagonal rings). (See Figure 7)   The dance continues tirelessly – partners meeting and separating over and over again.

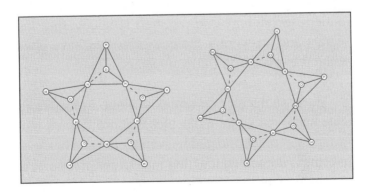

Fig. 7 Schematic Pentagonal and Hexagonal Water Rings

29

Although these diagrams were drawn in the 1970's, and are only *single plane* drawings, they still help to represent the predominant structures in liquid water.

Here, it is worth mentioning that the hexagonal shape of a snowflake and the hexagonal structuring of water are fundamentally different. Although one may be a reflection of the other, a snowflake is a fixed shape, composed of billions of water molecules, while the hexagonal water structure is a fluid, *momentary* combination of six simple water molecules.

Hexagonal Water – The Puzzle Solved

In athletic events, it is said that records exist only to be broken. Along this same line, "puzzles" exist only to be solved. The puzzle of water has been kept for a long time but it is finally being solved. Our modern technology and research is uncovering the secrets and answering the questions that have gone without explanation for many years.

Water molecules do not exist alone in the liquid state and even water molecules that are formed into groupings (predominated by pentagonal and hexagonal rings) are joined together into larger groups - via hydrogen bonding. In other words, water is an interconnected, mass of predominantly five and six-membered units, forming a unique lattice that gives water many of its unusual qualities.

Figure 8 is a representation of water, with groupings of pentagonal and hexagonal units joined as larger clusters in the mobile liquid state.

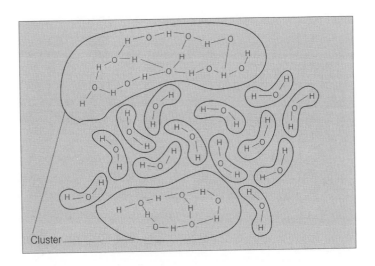

Fig. 8 ***Groupings of interconnected water molecules in the liquid state***

Temperature

Temperature is one of the factors that determines whether water combines to form hexagonal or pentagonal groups. When bulk water is examined to measure the proportion of hexagonally-shaped structures, temperature makes a big difference. At 10° C., 22% of water is hexagonally-shaped. However, at the freezing point (0° C.) 26% of water is hexago-

31

nally-shaped. (see Figure 9) And, somewhere between -30° and -40° C, water reaches the super-
cooled state where it is 100% hexagonally-structured. (see Figure 10)

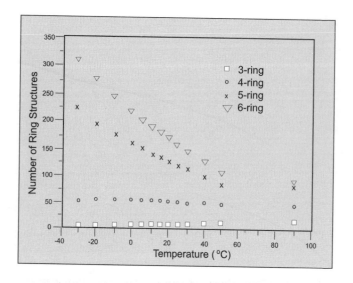

*Fig. 9 Water Structure as a function of Temperature
1000 water molecules were used and the data
were obtained by analyzing the trajectory collected for 20,000 steps of product dynamics at
each temperature.*

The Puzzle of Molecular Weight

In 1964, in conjunction with the world famous scientist, Dr. Henry Eyring (1901-1982), we presented a paper, titled, "The Significant Structure Theory of Water." In this paper, we proposed that the key to the unusual characteristics of water was found

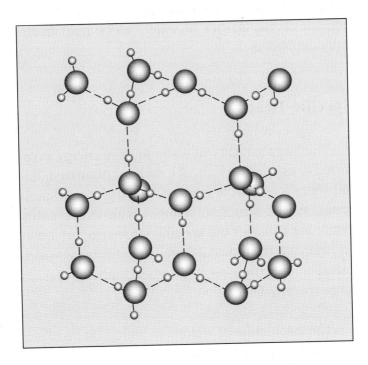

Fig. 10   100% Hexagonal Structuring of Water

in its structure. Accordingly, the molecular weight of water – $(H_2O)_2$ - generally accepted to be 18, ought to be calculated based on a combination of pentagonal and hexagonal groups which predominate in bulk water. In other words, water is comprised of different percentages of $(H_2O)5$ (molecular weight, 90) and $(H_2O)6$ (molecular weight, 108), depending on temperature. Using these revised molecular weights and an understanding of water structure, the unusual characteristics of water can be mathematically explained.

Specific Heat

The large capacity of water to store energy is referred to as specific heat. As we have discussed, liquid water is a mass of interconnected groups of molecules whose structure changes with temperature. When we consider the specific structuring of water and increase the molecular weight in formulas which calculate specific heat, we can account for water's large specific heat value.

The calculation of water's specific heat increases exponentially towards the direction of super-cooling at -40° C., where water is 100% hexagonally-structured. (see Figure11) Notice the difference in heat capacity between ice (26% hexagonally-structured) and super-cooling water (approaching100% hexagonally-structured) at the same temperatures.

Perhaps you have already figured out that the specific heat of Hexagonal Water is higher than that of pentagonal water. What this means is that Hexagonal Water has a greater capacity to perform work – to expel wastes, to absorb temperature changes and to protect against various other energetic influences. This has significant implications as we will see.

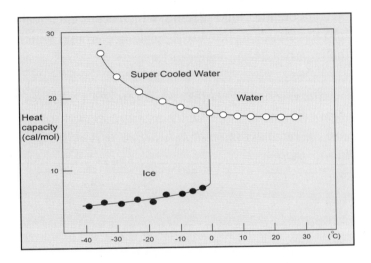

Fig. 11 The Specific heat of water and ice

What is Super-cooled Water?

An understanding of the super-cooled state is important to an understanding of structured water. Super-cooled water exists in a *liquid form*, even though the temperature of the water *is well below freezing*. The difference between ice and super-cooled water is like the difference between a still, smooth, sleeping ocean and one that is, awake and alive with movement.

The super-cooled state is best understood in terms of weather. Winter clouds contain super-cooled water, composed of tiny water droplets at below freezing temperatures which freeze *immediately* when they come in contact with *any* surface. Obviously, this poses a problem for aircraft during the winter and is the reason airplanes are de-iced before flying into clouds laden with super-cooled water. It is also the concept behind cloud seeding, which sends chemicals into the clouds to provide a substance around which the ice crystals can begin to form.

Super-cooled, 100% hexagonally-structured water has a huge capacity to store energy which can be released immediately when it is utilized by living matter.

100% hexagonally-structured water has a huge capacity to store energy which can be released immediately when it is utilized by living organisms.

Density

As we have shown, the density of water also changes peculiarly with temperature. With research, we have discovered that the hexagonal form of water, characterized by a more "open" structure, is less dense and has a greater volume. The pentagonal form is more tightly held together and takes up a smaller volume. This knowledge helps to explain the unusual density changes in water.

Ice, with a higher percentage of hexagonal structures is less dense than its liquid state, so it floats. However, as ice melts and the percentage of hexagonal structures decreases, density and volume also decrease. But as the temperature rises above of 4° C., the kinetic forces between molecules begins to cause enough vibrational heat movement that the distance between molecules increases as expected – eventually resulting in vaporization.

Figure 12 shows the density of water, super-cooled water and ice. If water were to follow a normal pattern, it would increase in density as the temperature decreases. However, because of the specific structure of water, its density reaches a peak at 4° C. and then expands as it freezes. The dotted line shows super-cooling water, with temperatures below freezing but still in the liquid state.

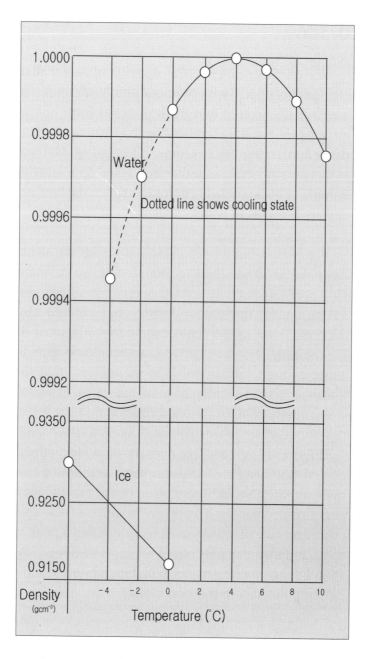

Fig. 12 Water Density as a function of temperature

Viscosity

Water's abnormal viscosity can also be explained at the molecular level when we consider the existence of water structuring. When pressure is exerted on water, it becomes less viscous (flows more easily). This is because pressure initially breaks the bonding that holds hexagonal structures together and forces a predominance of pentagonal structures, which are characterized by greater mobility. As the pressure is continually increased, free space between molecules decreases and viscosity begins to follow a more normal pattern.

Above 30° C. there is a relatively small proportion of Hexagonal Water, so viscosity does not change with pressure above this temperature.

Water – the Ultimate Energy Carrier and Waste Removal System

Water plays a very important role in discharging metabolic waste from the body. There is no other material that can perform this function in the same way. Since water has the capacity to hold so much energy, it is also the perfect means of energy transfer within biological systems. Obviously, Hexagonal Water has the greatest energetic capacity. Perhaps this is the reason that studies using melted snow water (with a high hexagonal content) have shown significant positive physiological responses in plant and animal growth.

Snow water is not merely cold water. It has an extremely high concentration of hexagonal structures, indicative of the super-cooling it has undergone prior to condensing into ice.

Water's Memory

Very recent studies indicate that water has the capacity to maintain the energy/frequency of a substance placed in it – even after the substance is removed. Processing with magnetic and electric fields is reported to enhance and even stabilize structural changes which can last for significant periods of time. It is also possible for water that has been hexagonally-structured at one time, to "remember" and assume this structure once inside the body. Accordingly, snow water, with a high degree of hexagonal structuring, can be considered a highly energetic water with the ability to activate and support numerous metabolic functions.

Processing with *magnetic* and *electric* fields is reported to enhance and even stabilize structural changes which can last for significant periods of time.

After all these years, the pieces of the water puzzle are coming together and what was once only a theory is being confirmed via a variety of methodologies, including NMR, X-ray diffraction, computer simulation, spectroscopy and other methods. Water has a specific structure which varies with environmental conditions. The fact that the study of Hexagonal Water is now an established field of science, is evidence of the theory's growing acceptance.

...what was once only a theory is being confirmed...

Water has a specific structure which varies with environmental conditions.

THE
WATER PUZZLE

Water Structure at Interfaces

Chapter

4

THE WATER PUZZLE

Chapter 4
Water Structure at Interfaces

Water and Ions

As water cascades down mountains, joining rivers and streams, it dissolves countless minerals. Thus, unless water has been distilled, it includes numerous dissolved solids. In the dissolved state, minerals and other materials can be carried in water without being visible. So, it is impossible to discuss water without a discussion of minerals.

Minerals dissolved in water are in the form of ions (charged particles). Sodium, Calcium, Magnesium, Chloride and Sulfide ions are among those typically found in water. It should be noted that water from different parts of the world contains different concentrations of ions because of the different minerals in the rocks and soil.

Water from the villages in the Caucasus Mountains in Russia is considered to be one of the best sources of water in the world. It contains numerous ions and comes from the snow-covered mountains that surround the villages. The populations of this part of the world have been studied again and again to discover why their inhabitants live such long and healthy lives. Perhaps the answer lies in the structure of the water and in the ions which are present in it. It is worth mentioning that the process during which super-cooled water freezes, is called *glaciation*. The glacial ice that forms the water supply for these villages is highly hexagonally-structured and contains numerous ions.

Structure-making vs. Structure-breaking ions

Ions and water structure affect the properties of water. If an ion is placed in distilled water, a powerful electric field is formed and the structure of the water near the ion is altered. Through the course of time, we have discovered that certain ions strengthen the hexagonal structure of water and other ions actually weaken this structure.

Table 2. Examples of Structure-making ions and Structure-breaking ions

Structure-making ions			Structure-breaking ions		
Name	Ion	^Eww*	Name	Ion	^Eww*
Calcium	Ca^{2+}	32.2	Magnesium	Mg^{2+}	-8.8
Lithium	Li^+	27.2	Potassium	K^+	-3.8
Sodium	Na^+	3.3	Rubidium	Rb^+	-6.3
Zinc	Zn^{2+}	50.6	Aluminum	Al^{3+}	-313.4
Iron	Fe^{3+}	51.9	Chloride	Cl^-	-7.5
Copper	Cu^{2+}	49.8	Bromide	Br^-	-7.5
Silver	Ag^+	4.2	Fluoride	F^-	-18.0
Nickel	Ni^{2+}	51.0	Iodide	I^-	-7.9
Molecular movement is made difficult due to the water molecule's decreased degree of freedom. *(Hexagonal Water increases)*			Molecular movement is facilitated due to the water molecule's increased degree of freedom. *(Pentagonal Water increases)*		

* ^**Eww** is the interaction energy (kJ/mol) between the water molecules in solution

Structure-making ions in solution have a positive interaction energy (^Eww). In other words, they hold water molecules tightly, so they are less likely to interact (move freely) than the water around *structure-breaking* ions. The greater the interaction energy, the greater the *structure-making* capacity.

The main factors that determine whether ions are *structure-making* or *structure-breaking* are:
· the interaction energy of the ions with water in the first hydration shell and

- the dimension of the ions - characterized by polarizability.

Of the alkali metals, Sodium and Lithium, (small atomic size), are *structure-making* ions, whereas Potassium, Rubidium and Cesium (larger atomic size) are *structure-breaking* ions. The halide ions (Cl^-, Fl^-, Br^- I^-) are all *structure-breaking* ions due to the change in the direction of the dipole because of their negative charge and the resulting expansion of the first hydration shell. And as for most multiple charged ions (Zn^{2+}, Ni^{2+}, Fe^{3+}), their strong attraction to the surrounding water molecules reduces the distance to molecules in the first hydration shell and they are tightly held. On the other hand, since Be^{2+}, Mg^{2+} and Al^{3+} are very small ions, and their interaction with water molecules is strong, they are continually exposed to the influence of bulk water and are not strongly held. These ions are considered *structure-breaking* ions. (see Figure 13)

Generally speaking, when the electric charge of an ion is large or when the ion has a small volume, hexagonal structure is weakened. These are called negatively hydrated ions. However, when the charge is relatively small or the size of the ion is larger, hexagonal structuring is encouraged. These are known as positively hydrated ions. **Structure-making, positively hydrated ions, strengthen the bonding between water molecules and increase the number of hexagonal structures in the water solution.**

In other words, Calcium, Sodium, Zinc, Iron, Silver, Copper and others, help to convert water into Hexagonal Water, while Potassium, Chloride, Fluoride, Aluminum, Sulfide etc., destroy the hexagonal structuring of water.

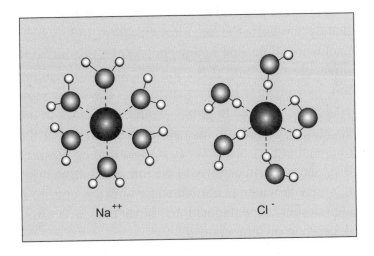

Fig. 13 Hydration of Sodium (Na²⁺) and Chlorine (Cl⁻)

Figure 13 shows the difference in the first hydration layer of a *structure-making* ion (Na^{2+}) and a *structure-breaking* ion (Cl^-). Here it is easy to see how certain ions can contribute to the structuring of the surrounding water and how others can disrupt it.

The Hydration of Ions

Water surrounds ions in a series of layers, called *hydration layers*. The nature of the way that each ion interfaces with individual water molecules, determines whether it is a *structure-making*, or a *structure-breaking* ion.

Figure 14 shows a schematic hydration model devised by Frank and Wen. In this Figure, the ion is *structure-making* and water molecules that are immediately bonded to the ion, form a uniform, tightly-held enclosure. The first hydration layer (A) is only one molecule thick and if the ion is a structure-making ion, that layer is highly structured - the water molecules are not free to move. Water molecules in the second layer, (B) are also structured, but not to the degree that they are in the first hydration layer, since they are not held directly to the ion. Hydration layer (C) or bulk water, is normal water with a proportionate number of pentagonal and hexagonal structures, depending on temperature.

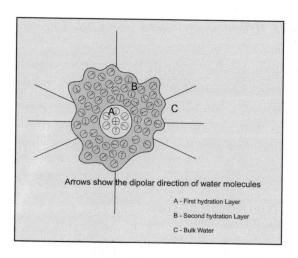

Arrows show the dipolar direction of water molecules

A - First hydration Layer

B - Second hydration Layer

C - Bulk Water

Fig. 14. Frank & Wen's Hydration Model

Figure 15 shows the hydration of the Lithium (Li^+) ion – a *structure-making* ion. This, 3-dimensional perspective shows the *uniform* tetrahedral structure formed by Lithium and its initial hydration layer.

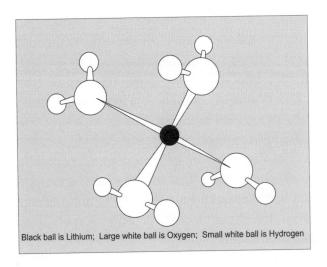

Black ball is Lithium; Large white ball is Oxygen; Small white ball is Hydrogen

Fig. 15. Hydration of the Lithium Ion

Water Structure and Ions Within the Body

Since scientists have not fully understood how to isolate and study the effects of water structure by itself, they have often turned their focus to the things that are found dissolved in water (ions). Of course, the answers are not found in either area alone, but in understanding the whole picture.

The fact that the structure between water molecules is strengthened by some ions, may account for the higher level of metabolic activity that ionized water supports in connection with biological organisms. Alkaline, ionized water, (one form of hexagonally-structured water) has a high concentration of *structure-making* ions. Research has shown that alkaline ionized water can slow the progression of cancer. (see chapter 5)

The Potassium ion (K^+) is one of the ions that breaks Hexagonal Water structure, while the Calcium ion (Ca^{2+}) strengthens it. The effects of these two ions on cellular activity can be partially understood by the way in which they affect the structure of water. Potassium accelerates the activity of neuromuscular cells, while Calcium can slow the proliferation of abnormal cells (as in cancer).

Certain other ions and biological molecules have been shown to strengthen the structure of water as well. Vitamin C and Germanium are two such substances. Both are known to play significant roles in preserving and maintaining health. It is likely that this is due, in part, to their role in supporting the hexagonal structure of water.

Calcium Within the Body

It is one thing to speculate on the interaction of ions in structured water and their function within the human body; it is quite another matter to show positive correlation through research and clinical trials. On this front, much remains to be done. However, it is possible to get a glimpse of the relationship by examining the function of ions at the cellular level. Many diseases that affect the elderly have been linked with mineral (ion) deficiencies.

For example, Dr. McCarron, who conducted research on the relationship between the amount of Calcium consumed and high blood pressure, came to the following conclusions:

- Cardiovascular disease is significantly reduced when water with a high Calcium concentration is consumed.
- High blood pressure can be stabilized by consuming a sufficient amount of Calcium.
- High blood pressure among pregnant women is under .5% when daily Calcium consumption exceeds 1000 mg. However, it increases to 1.0% when consumption is under 500 mg. daily.

There are many opinions regarding the mode of action of Calcium as it relates to blood pressure - everything from normalization of the parathyroid gland hormone secretory system to a direct effect on the contraction and relaxation of the blood vessels in smooth muscle. Whatever the case may be, Calcium also affects water structure. In this way, the Calcium ion effects biological functions directly as well as indirectly through its influence on water structure. This indirect influence may be just as important as any direct relationship we discover.

Electrolytes (ions) in Bodily Fluids

Even when we put the issue of water structure aside, there is a close relationship between ions and bodily functions. Figure 16, below, shows the proportion of ions in bodily fluids.

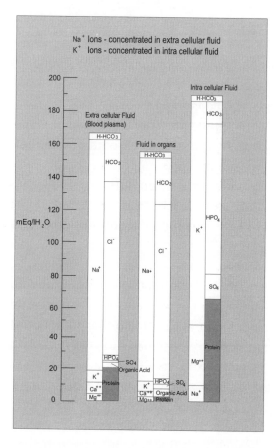

Fig. 16 Electrolytes (ions) in body fluids

As you can see, Sodium and Chloride ions are predominant outside the cell, (extra cellular fluid) while Potassium and Phosphoric Acid ions predominate the intra cellular fluid. The concentration and placement of Sodium and Potassium ions is involved in the *Action Potential* which refers to the electrical signals produced to open and close ion channels. This is a kind of pumping system that utilizes the positive and negative charges of ions to create tiny explosive forces which pump materials back and forth across the cellular membranes.

When the *structure-making/breaking* capacity of ions is considered along with their known functions, we may find that they have a broader influence on cellular activity than we have thought.

Water and Proteins

Biological systems do not function without water. Thus, a knowledge of the interaction of water with biomolecules (protein) is indispensable. Recently, my lab has been involved in the study of structured water and proteins. Using various methods of computer simulation, we have found that the water immediately surrounding normal protein forms a greater percentage of hexagonal structures. We have also found that the water surrounding abnormal (cancer-causing) proteins has a significantly decreased number of hexagonal structures and an increased number of pentagonal structures. Our studies have shown some interesting characteristics regarding how water interacts with the proteins of a variety of tissues in the human body.

> **... the water surrounding abnormal (cancer-causing) proteins has a significantly decreased number of hexagonal structures**

Layers of water

We have measured the state of the water next to functional biological molecules using several techniques, including: osmotic swelling coefficients, dielectric relaxation, NMR and Differential Scanning Calorimetry. Results show that there are 3 different layers or *states* to the water that surrounds these proteins. These layers are similar to the 3 hydration layers we found surrounding individual ions. When discussing proteins, these are referred to as the X, Y and Z water layers. (see Figure 17)

Water that is bonded directly with a functional protein is referred to as the Z layer and is so tightly held that it has an almost solid structure while maintaining the liquid state. The Y layer is an intermediate layer, followed by the X layer which is considered *bulk water.*

The water of these three states is characterized by different traits. Dielectric relaxation time (T) of the

Z-layer (bonded directly to the protein) is 10^{-5} to 10^{-7} seconds, exhibiting the high level of organization we have noted earlier and a solid-like structure. The water of this Z layer has a calculated freezing point of about -100 ° C. Obviously, this highly structured layer provides incredible thermal protection.

Relaxation time (T) of the Y layer is 10^{-9} seconds, indicative of some sort of organization, yet a more mobile state. The (T) of the X layer (ordinary bulk water) is 10^{-12} seconds. This indicates an active, mobile state of the water in this hydration layer.

We have conducted numerous calculations on the structure of the water surrounding various biological proteins. As an example, 62% of the water that im-

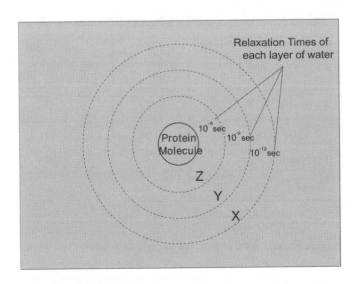

Fig. 17 Hydration of Proteins (X, Y, Z water)

mediately hydrates normal Alanine dipeptide is hex-agonally-shaped. 24% is pentagonally-shaped, and 14% is other structures.

Blood Plasma

A quick analysis of blood plasma indicates that the two major components are water and protein. Blood plasma is 90% water and 7% protein - yet for every protein there is an average of 70,000 water molecules which immediately surround it in a hydration layer one molecule deep. Metaphorically speaking, these water molecules act as servants to the larger protein molecules and they participate in a number of ways, structurally supporting the folds and bends which facilitate their function and protecting them from outside disturbances.

Table 3. Components of Blood Plasma

Component	Weight (%)	Average molecular weight	# of molecules per protein
Protein	7	10,000	1
Electrolytes	1	58	240
Organics	2	150	190
Water	90	18	70,000

Hexagonal Water and DNA

Let's take a look at the relationship between DNA and water. DNA is responsible for the genetic information of the body - it is the nucleus of life. Because both DNA and water are so fundamentally connected with life, this is a very profound area of research.

Figure 18 shows computer-generated models of normal and abnormal DNA. B-DNA (normal DNA) on the left is shaped as a clean helical spiral. However, Z-DNA (abnormal DNA) on the right is distorted.

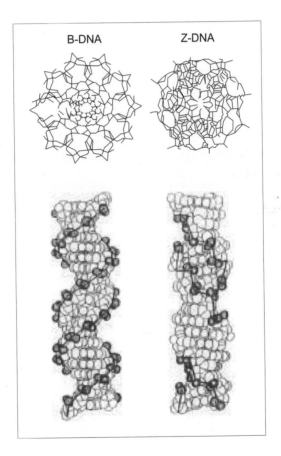

***Fig. 18 Multi-dimensional structure of B-DNA and
Z-DNA***

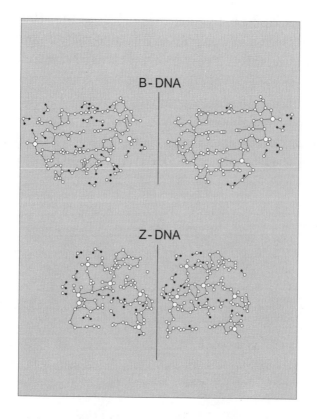

Fig.19 Stereoviews of the Hydration Structure of
B-DNA (normal) and Z-DNA (abnormal)

In our study of the hydration of DNA, we have
discovered that there are 36 water molecules bound
together in the first hydration layer surrounding B-
DNA. (Figure 19 - top) On the other hand, only 25
water molecules are found in this same hydration layer
surrounding Z-DNA. (Figure 19 - bottom). This supports another finding – that the water surrounding
normal DNA is highly structured, and much less mo-

bile than the water around abnormal DNA. This tightly-held and highly structured water which surrounds normal DNA acts to stabilize the helical structure of the DNA. It forms a layer of protection from all sorts of outside influences which could cause malfunction or distortion.

Water and Collagen

Collagen is the most abundant protein in the body. It is the major component of joints, cartilage, skin and connective tissue. It is responsible for the "cushion" in joints and the suppleness in the skin, which is largely due to the amount of water it holds. Water plays a unique role between the strands of collagen and although it is difficult to show in a 2-dimensional schematic drawing, we have found a layer of structured water between the helical strands of collagen. (see Figure 20)

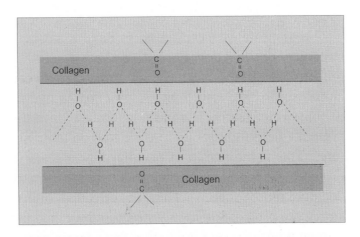

Fig. 20 State of Water Between Strands of Collagen

Generally speaking, the water molecules in the hydration layers surrounding any healthy protein are not free – they are held tightly by "authoritative' proteins in an almost servant/master relationship. In so doing, this highly structured water protects and supports an infinite number of biological processes.

Thermal Protection of Proteins

Protein is known to deteriorate and lose function when temperature and/or pressure increases. However, there are some microorganisms that exist in very high temperatures – without damage. One such organism, found in the vicinity of a Mediterranean volcanic vent, has an optimal growing temperature of 100° C. Using computer simulation, we looked at the interaction between water and the proteins of this unique microorganism.

These proteins were found to have a stronger structure - one that does not unfold as easily as other proteins due to a stronger electrical attraction between amino acids. We also found a grouping of hydrophobic (water-fearing) amino acids at the core of the protein - held tightly due to their hydrophobic nature. This combination of peculiarities appears to protect them from temperatures that would normally denature other proteins. Thus, the effects of highly structured protein and highly structured water at the protein interface were protecting these microorganisms from heat damage.

Another study of a similar nature was conducted on the proteins of the Winter Flounder that inhabit polar regions. These proteins, known as *anti-freeze proteins*, are resistant to the exceptionally cold temperatures of the water they inhabit. According to the results of this study, a specific amino acid binds ice crystals near the surface of the protein and other hydrophobic amino acids contribute by keeping water molecules from approaching the surface of the protein. This results in a lower freezing point immediately around the proteins and a slower formation of ice crystals. These fish are then able to survive the freezing temperatures of the water they inhabit.

Are you beginning to see how water interfaces with other substances? Some substances (whether simple ions or huge protein molecules) interact with water in a manner that supports the Hexagonal Water structure. They can be said to be positively hydrated and the water immediately surrounding them is hexagonally-structured.

Other substances, for various reasons, (structural configuration, size, electrostatic charge, etc.) tend to be surrounded by water of a lesser structure. These substances are said to be negatively-hydrated or hydrophobic.

The fact that healthy DNA is positively hydrated and abnormal DNA is negatively hydrated is a big clue to the importance of Hexagonal Water in the molecular environment. And when we find that cancerous and non-cancerous cells exhibit a similar hydration phenomenon (see chapter 5) the astute mind will begin to see how the pieces of the puzzle come together.

> **Some substances interact with water in a manner that supports the Hexagonal Water structure.**
>
> **Other substances, tend to be surrounded by water of a lesser structure.**

THE
WATER PUZZLE

Hexagonal Water & Human Health

Chapter

5

THE WATER PUZZLE

Chapter 5
Hexagonal Water and Human Health

The Molecular Water Environment Theory

In 1986, at a symposium in the United States on cancer, I presented the *molecular water environment theory* to a group of scientists. Dr. Albert Szent-Györgyi, the man who discovered Vitamin C and a Nobel Prize Laureate, commended the theory and encouraged the work, saying that if it could be proven, it would be a landmark in science. Since the early 1990's, research has begun to prove this theory, which proposes that:

Replenishing the Hexagonal Water in our bodies, can:
- *increase vitality,*
- *slow the aging process*
- *and prevent disease*

Drinking Hexagonal Water is the only realistic way of replenishing this vital component of our bodies, so the question becomes, "How do we create Hexagonal Water for regular consumption?"

Methods of Producing Hexagonal Water

There are a number of conditions that favor the production of hexagonally-structured water. The first is temperature and as we have noted, when the temperature drops, the percentage of hexagonal structures increases. We have also noted that it is possible to achieve a state where water is 100% hexagonally structured, as in the super-cooled state or where water is tightly held to biological molecules.

Another condition that favors Hexagonal Water is the existence of *structure-making* ions. When ions such as Calcium are added to pure water, the percentage of hexagonal ring-structures increases. This is a good reason for drinking water with dissolved minerals, as long as the proportion of *structure-making* minerals exceeds that of the *structure-breaking* minerals.

Other conditions known to influence the structure of water are strong energetic fields. Two known methods currently fall into this class - the use of electric or magnetic fields. Perhaps the most well known is ionization – otherwise know as electrolyzation. In this process, water is placed in an electric field and the positive ions in the water are pulled to one side of a permeable membrane while the negative ions are drawn to the other side. This procedure produces alkaline water on one side and acidic water on the other. The electric current is a powerful force for structuring water, however the stability of the resultant water can be short-lived and water must be consumed within a specified period of time after ionization in order to assure the hexagonal structure.

As with the use of electric current, the use of strong magnetic fields also influences water structure. In some studies, magnetic fields (.1 volts/A) were able to increase the concentration of Hexagonal Water up to 80%, verified by computer simulation. Another study showed that magnetically-produced Hexagonal Water had an increased concentration of dissolved oxygen. The magnetic production of Hexagonal Water has been very successful for creating stabilized, hexagonally-structured water, suitable for human consumption.

Three methods of producing Hexagonal Water:
1. **Lowering temperatures**
2. **The addition of *structure- making* ions**
3. **Using outside energetic fields such as:**
   · **Ionization (also called electrolyzation)**
   · **The use of strong magnetic fields**

Aging and the Molecular Water Environment

In English, there is an expression, "the water of life," which implies the importance of water to life. Conversely, the term, "withered" has been used to describe the lack of water in the aged. Water and aging are directly related and it has been shown that the water content of the body decreases with age, producing a visible wrinkling and withering effect. Keep in mind that the outward signs of aging are just an indicator of what is also happening on the inside of the body. At the cellular level, aging causes a shift in the ratio of water inside vs. outside the cell. The volume of water inside the cell is reduced and cells "wither" just like the skin on the outside of the body.

Infants are approximately 80% water by weight, yet it is not uncommon for the amount of water in the elderly to be below 50%. Figure 21 compares the amount of bodily fluid by age.

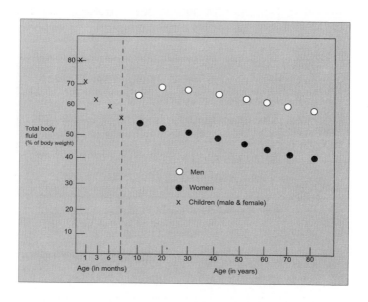

Fig. 21   Comparison of body fluid by age

Cell Water Turnover

The amount of water discharged from the body on a daily basis, is also dependant on age - and gender. Generally speaking, an adult male will both consume and discharge 30 ml. of water for each kg. of body weight (approx. 2.5 liters for a 175 lb. man). Women consume and discharge 25 ml. for the same kg. of body weight. This amount decreases with age and the total amount of body water decreases. (see Table 4)

Table 4.　Water Excretion by Age

Age	1st year	5 years	10 years	Young man	Young woman
Excretion (ml/kg)of body wt.	125-150	100	75	30	25

The younger a person is, the greater the amount of total water movement or *cell water turnover* they experience. Newborn babies experience the fastest water turnover of any stage in life. They also experience the most active metabolism. Hence, the metabolic rate has been correlated with the amount of cell water turnover in the body and both have been linked with health and aging. When seen from this perspective, *cell wa-*

ter turnover becomes an important marker for over-
all health and longevity.

> **Metabolic rate has been correlated with the amount of cell water turnover in the body - both have been linked with health and aging.**

One of the things that Hexagonal Water has clearly been shown to improve is cell water turnover. Smaller hexagonal units, as opposed to larger, unorganized conglomerates of water, are able to penetrate cells more rapidly, having an overall effect on metabolism, nutrient absorption, waste removal, etc. This increased rate of cell water turnover can be measured with non-invasive Bio Impedance instruments.

Children are much more vulnerable to the loss of water. The requirement for water to support their higher metabolic rate is much greater than for adults. This is why even slight diarrhea can cause dehydration among children.

The elderly are also vulnerable – but for a different reason. As people age, their bodies dry out and total body water decreases. Intracellular water (water inside the cells) decreases and bodily functions begin to slow down. At the same time the thirst sensation decreases. In the elderly, the *triggers for water replacement* (thirst and metabolic rate) do not function as well and the elderly tend to consume less and less water. Their water reserves are typically lower and their vulnerability to water loss increases.

Aging is a Loss of Structured Water

Magnetic Resonance Imaging (MRI) has shown that not only is there a decrease in total body water with age, but that there is also a difference in the amount of *structured* water in the body from infancy to old age. According to the molecular water environment theory:

**Aging is a loss of Hexagonal Water
from organs, tissues and cells,
and
an overall decrease in total body water.**

Since aging is associated with the loss of Hexagonal Water from the body, it has been suggested that consuming Hexagonal Water results in a general slowing of the aging process. Several studies support this premise.

The Issue of Weight

Often, aging is associated with an increase in weight (which has sometimes been misinterpreted as excess water). In reality, the overweight individual has a reduced amount of total body water – up to 20% less than a normal individual. Since age, metabolic rate and water structure are directly related, the fact that overweight individuals have a reduced metabolic rate and a reduced amount of total body water, indicates the potential for resolve with increasing amounts of Hexagonal Water.

Hexagonal Water Supports Metabolic Efficiency

Water is the medium in which bodily functions take place and our research has shown that it is Hexagonal Water that is biologically preferred. Hexagonal Water supports metabolic efficiency and is associated with other positive functional activities within the body. We have also shown that pentagonal water is associated with cancer, diabetes and other abnormal conditions.

There are numerous reasons why Hexagonal Water is the choice when it comes to supporting a long and healthy life. One of these is the amount of energy carried in Hexagonal Water - characterized by specific heat. If you recall from chapter 3, when we took into account the structuring of water, we were able to understand why water had such a high degree of specific heat. In other words we could account for the ability of water to hold a great deal more energy than expected. Hexagonal Water has a larger caloric capacity and a greater ability to perform "work." It is the obvious biological choice.

> **Hexagonal Water is energetically more powerful.**
> **It is the obvious biological choice.**

One of the biggest problems for any biological organism, is the removal of waste from the system. Every metabolic function produces waste which causes acidification (hardening) of organs and tissues. Over-acidification has been correlated with both disease and aging and if an organism can eliminate wastes more efficiently, its life expectancy and overall health will be enhanced.

Since water has such a high energetic capacity, and since it has the ability to dissolve matter, it is the logical candidate for clean up. When considering the differences between pentagonal and Hexagonal Water, **Hexagonal Water is the preferred choice**. *It is energetically more powerful*! Hexagonal Water improves cell water turnover and supports metabolic efficiency. In this way, it helps to prevent illness and has the potential to delay aging.

The Water of Longevity

It is said that people who live long, do so because of favorable living conditions - they enjoy longevity since their environment is more natural and favorable compared to other environments. We have mentioned that the longevity of people in certain parts of the world may be due to the kind of water they drink. In these areas, the year-round supply of water comes from permanent snow fields. Not only is the percentage of hexagonal structures in this water, very high but it also contains a balance of dissolved ions. The water consumed in these parts of the world has been super-cooled and then frozen for long periods of time. Drinking this Hexagonal *snow water* appears to support greater health, enhanced immune function, increased metabolic activity and slower aging.

The Relationship Between Survival and Hexagonal Water

A long time ago, Verhulst suggested that the relationship between survival rate and survival time for all living organisms followed an S-shaped curve and outlined life or death as a probability.

This survival curve can be explained effectively in terms of the loss of Hexagonal Water inside the body. For example, Figure 22 shows the survival rate of 32 beagle dogs (excluding instances of accidental death). The left and right sides show dogs with inborn disease and normal (control) dogs, respectively. The stair steps in the graph were calculated based on the proportion of hexagonally-structured water in the body and the amount of disordered water being discharged from the body. Smooth lines are a calculation using the "molecular water environment theory" which assumes a proportionate decrease of structured water with age.

In this research, more than half of the dogs that retained an extensive amount of structured water in their bodies survived over 13 years. On the other hand, half of the dogs with a high percentage of un-structured water survived less than 7 years. In this study, the data (stair-stepped line) agree with the molecular water environment theory model (smooth line).

Here, z displays the time in which survival rate of each small group is halved, the proportion of Hexagonal Water in the body, is expressed as p, and the proportion of disordered water, discharged from the body, is shown as q. Given this information, the survival rate can be expressed by using the chemical reaction theory model. Experience has determined the survival rate formula as follows:

$$P=S=1/1+\exp[k(z-t)]$$

Here, $p+q = 1$. To calculate the S-shaped curve of Figure 1,

$z = 2335$ and $k = 1.86 \times 10^{-3}$ for the group of diseased dogs, and

$z = 4778$ and $k = 1.77 \times 10^{-3}$ for the group of normal dogs.

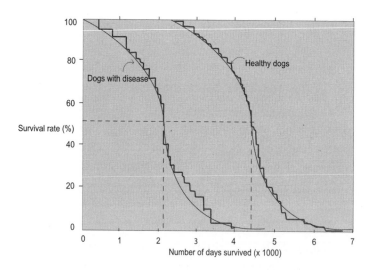

*Fig. 22 Survival as a function of Age and Hexago-
nal Water content*

Water, Calcium and Aging

According to the *molecular water environment
theory*, aging is a loss of structured water from the body
and an increase in the amount of disorganized water
that is discharged from the body via the bladder and
bowel. Human beings are more vulnerable to illnesses
as they age but even the elderly can maintain health and
vitality when the amount of Hexagonal Water in the
body is high. On the other hand, if the amount of pentagonal water is high, acidic wastes build up, metabolic
functions decrease and aging is accelerated.

> **Even the elderly can maintain health and
> vitality when the amount of
> Hexagonal Water in the body is high.**

78

It is also well-known that the loss of Calcium is a problem for the elderly and it is interesting that Calcium supplementation is frequently recommended as a treatment for many illnesses that afflict the elderly. Recall that the Calcium ion is considered a *structure-making* ion, so that when Calcium is present in water, the percentage of hexagonal structures increases.

Aging is a process of losing hexagonally-structured water which ultimately leads to the loss of Calcium. Theoretically, youth can be prolonged if these two factors can be prevented. The *molecular water environment theory* shows how aging can be deterred by preventing the loss of water and Calcium at the same time. This theory can be explained as follows:

The *structure-making* character of Calcium contributes to the formation of Hexagonal Water. At the same time, Hexagonal Water has an affinity for Calcium in the body. This is like saying that Hexagonal Water resonates with Calcium such that the possibility of losing Calcium from the cellular make-up decreases when there is a sufficient amount of Hexagonal Water.

In a similar manner, Hexagonal Water resonates with the major amino acids responsible for cell structure. (They are *structure-making* substances). Accordingly, the joint presence of Hexagonal Water and *structure-making* amino acids, helps to maintain cellular integrity and function throughout the body.

Healthy, supported cells have the power to balance ions within and without the cellular structure. When seen from this perspective, it is much easier to understand the interdependent relationship between Calcium and Hexagonal Water, both of which decrease with age.

Osteoporosis

Osteoporosis is an illness that afflicts the elderly, especially women. This is a disease where bones become brittle and vulnerable to fracture due to the loss of Calcium. The possible causes of osteoporosis have been cited as insufficient Calcium during youth, lack of exercise and hormonal imbalances occurring with menopause. However, its basic cause is largely unknown and there are no effective ways to prevent it. In order to slow the progression of this disease, the medical profession has used Calcium supplementation, and encouraged weight-bearing exercise and improvements in diet (away from too much protein and fat). Each of these methods reduces acidic waste (one of the functions of structured water) and helps to balance body chemistry (pH).

Given what we know about Calcium and Hexagonal Water, it is difficult to expect significant improvement in osteoporosis by adding Calcium alone. For those with osteoporosis, Calcium supplementation often merely results in an increase of Calcium discharged from the body – like pouring water into a container with no bottom. According to the *molecular water environment theory*, it is necessary to consume

Hexagonal Water along with Calcium so that it can be used more efficiently at the cellular level.

Hexagonal Water Prevents Illness

There is an old saying, "The time to fix the barn is before the cow is dead." Obviously, any attempts to make repairs to the body, should be considered before disease strikes. After that time, repairs are more difficult and death is often inevitable – too late to "fix the barn."

It is now an accepted fact that disease prevention is just as important as treatment. Health maintenance and disease prevention are finally gaining academic acceptance. At one time, a research company in the UK, studied the cost of prevention vs. the cost of disease treatment. The outcome of the study showed that prevention was a mere 1/16 of the total cost of treating disease. This is a great incentive for employing the best methods available to **prevent** illness. Hexagonal Water is a good place to begin a health maintenance program. Not only has it been used as a preventative measure, but it has even been used as an effective *treatment* for many health conditions.

In the human body, structured and disordered water exist at the same time and we have shown that the body's survival rate decreases as the amount of disordered water accumulates. The greater the amount of structured water in the body, the healthier an individual is and it is not likely that disease will invade the healthy body. Once again, an important *key* to health is the amount of hexagonally-structured water we have in our bodies. In the end, **the one with the most Hexagonal Water, wins!**

Dr. Gyu Hwan Choi of the National University School of Medicine in Seoul, Korea and I conducted a clinical study to determine the effect of alkaline ionized water (Hexagonal Water produced via ionization) on bodily functions. Our purpose was to verify the effect of Hexagonal Water on the treatment of constipation in a clinical setting. In this study, eight patients, suffering from chronic constipation, drank alkaline ionized water for four weeks. Bowel movement frequency and transition time (verified by X-ray) were monitored. At the same time, 34 control subjects (with regular bowel movements) drank the same water. Results showed several things:

1. Within 4 weeks, bowel movement frequency increased for six of the eight patients and the feeling of discomfort disappeared.
2. The average frequency of bowel movements for those with chronic constipation, went from 1.4 times/week ($\pm$ .6) to 2.7 times ($\pm$1.6).
3. The average transition time before drinking the water was 2 to 4 times longer than normal. After 4 weeks, the transition time improved by 40 to 60%.
4. The 34 regular (control) subjects who also drank alkaline ionized water showed no significant change.

In the published paper on this study, Dr. Choi explained the following: "The results of this study are the final fruits which show the effects of structured water on illnesses. However, since the structure of the human body is very intricate, more clinical studies are needed to prove the "molecular water environment theory."

Although the results of this study are limited to the use of alkaline ionized water for the treatment of constipation, the results have a broader significance. When constipation is prolonged, it affects many other functions in the body - from digestive processes to the functioning of various organs. Chronic constipation can lead to many forms of disease. Being able to effectively treat constipation is synonymous with the ability to **prevent** a wide array of health problems by maintaining an environment in the intestines that is not conducive to disease.

Hexagonal Water Enhances the Immune System

The immune system refers to the body's ability to resist and fight infection. We are born with a partially developed immune system, complete with antibodies transferred from mother and enhanced by the additional benefits of breast feeding. There are also instances, such as vaccination, where we create an artificial immune response. Historical records indicate that crude vaccines were used in clinical settings as early as 120 B.C. and the Chinese used a primitive vaccine, for the control of small pox before the 10th Century. From a broad perspective, vaccinations are a form of preventative medicine, although they are not always without side effects. A healthy immune response, whether naturally or artificially induced, is important for good health. Unfortunately, our immune systems are under constant attack and many incurable diseases seem to have the upper hand in today's world.

Normally, when a virus infiltrates the human body, it creates toxins which are circulated via the blood. Antibodies are created by the immune system and sent out into the body – also through the blood. If the antibodies are successful in destroying the virus, we are victorious. These antibodies remain in the blood for some time against the possibility of another similar attack and we say that we have developed immunity to a specific virus. However, if the immune system is not prepared to respond quickly or with enough force, we become sick.

When the body is under stress and the immune system is weak, it is not always able to overcome the attack of pathogenic substances. This can sometimes lead to disease. The causes of disease are usually linked to stress – in one form or another. Stresses can be chemical, environmental, emotional or any combination of these but they all weaken the immune system and from the standpoint of the "molecular water environment theory," they destroy the structure of Hexagonal Water in the body.

Stress changes Hexagonal Water (harmonious with biological systems) into pentagonal water, which is not recommended for the human body. In the end, metabolic activity decreases and the immune system is weakened.

Stress changes Hexagonal Water into pentagonal water, which is not recommended for the human body.

Vitamin C and Hexagonal Water

One of the factors that has been shown to enhance immune function is Vitamin C. Volumes of research have been conducted in an attempt to categorize the many and varied functions of this vitamin, however we still do not completely understand how vitamin C is able to strengthen the immune system. It has demonstrated effectiveness against many types of viral and bacterial infections and it has been shown to increase both the number and mobility of specialized white blood cells.

According to the *molecular water environment theory*, one of the ways that Vitamin C enhances the immune system is by affecting the structure of the water at the cellular level. Like Calcium and other *structure-making* ions, Vitamin C increases the amount of Hexagonal Water. In other words, because Vitamin C is a *structure-making* substance, it has an indirect effect on numerous cellular functions, including immune function.

Computer simulation research has been conducted to test Vitamin C's influence on molecular water structure. Results showed that at 25° C. (77° F.) for every 1 pentagonal structure, there was .553 hexagonal structures in pure water. However, after the addition of Vitamin C (222:1), hexagonal structures increased to .606 for every 1 pentagonal structure. This is significant evidence that Vitamin C can indirectly enhance immune function by altering the structure of the water at the cellular level.

Diabetes and Cancer

According to research conducted by Boyland, (published in the Proceedings of the Israel Academy of Sciences and Humanities) only 5% of cancers have physical origins such as radiation damage; another 5% are caused by viruses; while 90% are caused by chemicals in the environment. Most of these carcinogenic chemicals enter the body through breathing, eating and drinking and many are carried in water.

Diabetes and cancer are two modern illnesses which have proven to be very difficult to treat. Both are considered to be very complex and to have a number of causes. However, when the water environment of both diseases is evaluated, there are some commonalities which deserve further investigation.

Using the NMR proton spin-lattice relaxation method, it has been found that protons in the water surrounding malignant cells have a longer spin-lattice relaxation time than protons in the water around normal cells. (see Table 5) The same kind of correlation has been found when studying diabetic beta cells. In other words, the water environment of both cancerous and diabetic cells is less structured and the surrounding water is able to move more freely than the water around normal cells. Accordingly, **both cancer and diabetes have a common feature – the destruction of water structure at the cellular level.**

Table 5. **Comparison of Spin-lattice Relaxation times (T1) between normal and cancerous cells of various organs (100MHz NMR)**

Organ or tissue	Relaxation time for cancerous cells	Relaxation time for normal cells
Breast	1.080 ± .080	.367 ± .079
Skin	1.047 ± 1.108	.616 ± .019
Stomach	1.238 ± .109	.765 ± .075
Small intestine	1.122 ± .040	.641 ± .080
Liver	.832 ± .012	.570 ± .029
Spleen	1.113 ± .006	.701 ± .045
Lungs	1.110 ± .057	.788 ± .063
Lymphatic tissue	1.004 ± .056	.720 ± .076
Bone	1.027 ± .152	.554 ± .027
Bladder	1.241 ± .165	.891 ± .061
Nerve	1.204	.557 ± .158
Ovary	1.282 ± .118	.989 ± .004
Prostate	1.110	.803 ± .014

It has been suggested that the water environment plays a significant role in both cancer and diabetes and it is interesting to note that both these diseases have theoretical causes which are also somewhat similar.

Cancer is characterized by the fact that some cells in the body start replicating in an uncontrolled manner. Experimental experience indicates that cancer is connected with some sort of damage to the genetic code or to some change in the DNA itself. We have already discussed the role of water surrounding normal and abnormal DNA and we have shown that the water surrounding abnormal DNA is less structured.

Current theories for the cause of cancer indicate that genetic changes occur due to one of the following models:
1. The immunological model
2. The virus model
3. The somatic (cellular) mutation model
4. The genetic reading error model and
5. The proton-tunneling model

On a cellular or subcellular level, there are certain similarities between the proposed causes of cancer and those of diabetes. Consider the following:
1. Diabetes beta cells can be damaged during *autoimmune* reactions.
2. *Virus* either destroys or causes the malfunction of beta cells.
3. *Environmental chemicals* damage beta cells or cause their malfunction.

4. Hereditary factors reduce the amount of insulin and bring about a different water environment in and around beta cells and insulin receptors.

Interestingly, insulin is a hydrophilic (water-loving) and water *structure-making* substance – more support for the fact that the water environment of diabetic beta cells is less structured than that of normal cells.

In scientific research, the presence of water is often taken for granted and ignored, however, it plays an essential role in all biological functions and is especially critical for diabetic and cancer patients. The failure to consider its impact during disease, may be a glaring oversight.

One of the unusual characteristics of water, as mentioned earlier, is its ability to *temper* or *tone down* the effects of temperature changes in the environment. In a similar manner, water protects the cells of the body from environmental changes. It has been noted that when the hexagonal structure of the water near cells is compromised, the cells are more vulnerable to external stimuli. Ultimately, cells surrounded by less structured water are weaker and more prone to malfunction and genetic mutation.

Using High-directional Monte Carlo simulations, we were able to show the differing percentages of ring structures surrounding normal and malignant human proteins. Table 6 shows the results.

Table 6. The Occurrence (%) of ring structures in the water environment surrounding human oncogene proteins

Structure size	Normal p21/GDP	Cancerous p21/GDP
3-ring	13.67	14.52
4-ring	24.83	29.26
5-ring	26.32	31.75
6-ring	35.18	24.46

During this same study, we determined the distance of these hydrogen-bonded rings from the center of the proteins. Figure 23 shows the number and distance of each cyclic ring type in association with both cancerous and normal protein.

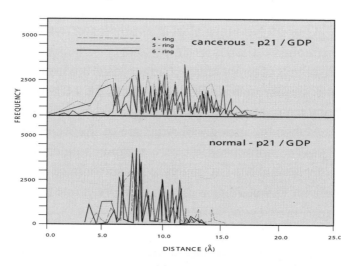

Fig. 23. Frequency and distribution of various ring-shaped water molecules in human oncogene proteins.

Each legend indicates the water network showing water molecules of corresponding number as a function of distance from the center of GDP.

Based on these and other findings that confirmed the presence of Hexagonal Water in greater proportion near normal (non-cancerous) proteins, many have suggested the possibility of returning cancer or diabetes cells to the normal state by improving the water environment at the cellular level. We joined Japan's Medical School to test this hypothesis.

Using methods for producing Hexagonal Water, we determined the effect of structured water on cultured cancer cells. Tumor cell culture (3T331) was grown on MEM culture medium and divided into 3 groups.

1. Control group – using unprocessed water
2. Test group 1 – using water with *structure-making* Calcium and *structure-breaking* Chloride ions added (as 25 mM $CaCl_2$)
3. Test group 2 – using hexagonally structured, alkaline ionized water made using 25 mM $CaCl_2$ – (since the electrolytic process separates positive and negative ions, the resultant water was structured and contained only the Calcium ion)

Figure 24 shows the results. In unprocessed water, tumor cells increased to 3.2 million in four days. However, the tumor cells that were exposed to alkaline ionized water decreased to 20,000 during the same 4-day period of time. This decrease could have been the effect of the Calcium ions themselves without the

91

structured water, which is the reason we introduced the same amount of Calcium as $CaCl_2$ in unstructured water.

Unfortunately, these kinds of tests cannot be performed inside the human body. However, this test shows the influence of Hexagonal Water and indicates a rather high possibility that the consumption of appropriately processed Hexagonal Water could slow the proliferation of cancer cells.

In our experience, we have found that when individuals consume Hexagonal Water, the cellular water environment improves, contributing to increased health. There are a number of reports which indicate that Hexagonal Water has halted the progression of cancer and disease. In light of our findings, this does not seem improbable, and yet clinical studies are still lacking.

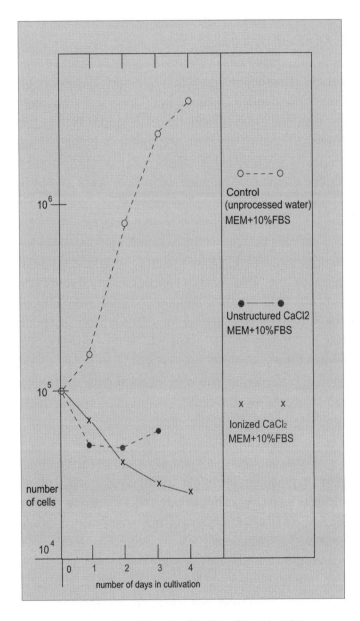

*Figure 24 The Effect of Alkaline Ionized Water on
Tumor Cell Growth*

Only when balance is maintained, does the water both in and outside cells retain a consistent structure, providing protection from various stresses and disturbances. In other words, when cells such as cancer cells become separated from the body's normal adjustment mechanisms (one of which is Hexagonal Water) they lose their ability to resist environmental changes and stress. Consumption of Hexagonal Water appears to rectify the natural balance within the body and *many* illnesses have been noted to improve.

The fact that the water near malignant cells is less structured, has lead to the use of cryotherapy or cryosurgery. This form of cancer therapy freezes cancer cells with minimal damage to the surrounding tissue. Cryotherapy is just one of 3 cancer treatment methods now being investigated which leverage the concepts of the *molecular water environment theory*. The second treatment method involves the use of ionized (electrolyzed) water, and the third, uses magnetically processed Hexagonal Water.

Within the cell itself, the structure of the water appears to play a major role in maintaining normal physiological activity. This is powerful evidence that the structure of the water plays an important role in cellular activity. Changes in the cell induce changes in the molecular water environment, both in and around the cell. When Hexagonal Water is introduced, it appears to improve the molecular water environment on a cellular level, contributing to a reduction in cancer cell growth and an increase in health. Recent clinical research has shown the same for diabetes, where blood sugar levels move in the direction of normalization with the regular consumption of Hexagonal Water.

A Strategy for Beating AIDS

AIDS emerged as a global issue in the 1980's and while many experts agree that only a vaccine can eliminate AIDS, the development of such a vaccine is considered very complex. One of the reasons for this is that the AIDS virus has the ability to transform or mutate – constantly changing and shifting - making a defense against it, like shooting at a moving target.

Normally, when a virus attacks, it infiltrates the cells, forcing them to duplicate the virus rather than to follow normal cellular duplication routines. When the immune system is functioning properly, variant cells are identified and eliminated in a timely manner. However, the AIDS virus attacks the very part of the immune system that is responsible for detection and elimination of foreign matter, the T-cells. The more T-cells that are destroyed, the more the virus is allowed to replicate without resistance, and the body is left defenseless. If the virus is allowed to take hold, the downhill battle of AIDS ensues and without a fully functional immune system, the body cannot resist the simple bacteria, molds and fungi that healthy individuals resist successfully on a daily basis. This is why most individuals with AIDS, die of secondary infections.

One of the interesting things about HIV is that many people can be carriers yet never contract the disease itself. Why is this? Because their immune systems are functioning properly and the virus cannot take hold. In other words, if an individual is healthy, with a fully functional immune system, HIV never develops into AIDS.

Recent evidence based on research from the University of Alabama, suggests that HIV was originally contracted from African chimpanzees, who carry the virus but are never affected. This evidence suggests that either their immune systems are healthy or that they have some natural resistance.

As human beings, the question is, how do we keep our immune systems fully functional? There are many factors, not the least of which is water. **An examination of cells infected with HIV reveals the same water environment as those with cancer and diabetes – a lack of organized structure at the cellular level.**

No clinical research has yet been conducted, using Hexagonal Water for AIDS. However, given the evidence already presented, it is not unreasonable to believe that because of its effects on metabolic function and on the immune system, Hexagonal Water could play a key role in the prevention of AIDS.

An examination of cells infected with HIV reveals the same water environment as those with cancer and diabetes – a lack of organized structure at the cellular level.

Water and Digestion

As a child, my grandfather taught me to drink a cup of cold water every morning before breakfast. My body shivered with a refreshing sensation as I drank the cold water from the well, since I had been told that "faucet water" was not good. Although I do not recall that my grandfather gave me a reason, I assumed that we drank the water to help digestion and to avoid constipation. I admired my grandfather greatly, and continued to follow his wise counsel for a long time. Today, I understand the science behind the folklore which claimed that cold water was highly beneficial for the body and helpful for good digestion.

In the 1970's Japan's Ministry of Health, Labor and Welfare officially announced that alkaline ionized water was effective for the resolution of abnormal fermentation in the intestines. Today, in Japan, this form of Hexagonal Water is known and used as a treatment for constipation.

Both constipation and diarrhea can result from abnormal fermentation in the intestines which is characterized by bowel movements with an exceptionally bad odor. Japanese research in this area has lead to a theory which claims that individuals who have chronically foul-smelling bowel movements are more prone to all kinds of disease. Their theory is based on the following:

- Various types of microorganisms inhabit the digestive tract. These microorganisms play roles in many functions such as digestion, nutrient absorption, detoxification, and immune function.

· Bowel movements have a foul odor when food is fermented by microorganisms in the intestinal tract.

· Fermentation affects the balance of microorganisms in the intestinal tract in an adverse manner – destroying beneficial bacteria and favoring unhealthy bacteria and yeasts.

· When microorganisms are kept in balance, clean-smelling bowel movements result.

· Fermentation in the intestinal tract is influenced by water quality, which is why alkaline ionized water has been shown to effectively treat constipation and reduce the fermentation in the intestinal tract.

According to this line of reasoning, fermentation (indicated by excessively bad-smelling bowel movements) points to an increased risk of many types of illness, including cancer, liver disease, diabetes, etc. and *water quality can make a difference.*

There are clinical studies that show that Hexagonal Water is an effective treatment for chronic constipation. Earlier, we discussed Dr. Choi's study, which was widely publicized in Japan and Korea.

Japanese experts, in an attempt to answer the question, "What type of water is best to drink?" came to the following conclusions:

1. Drink water which is free of harmful substances. One of the main reasons for fermentation in the intestinal tract is the use of chlorine which indiscriminately destroys microorganisms in the digestive tract and upsets the balance of intestinal flora. (However, they also determined that water which is boiled for many hours is also not appropriate for drinking).
2. Drink water that contains a balance of essential minerals (Distilled water that removes harmful substances and dissolved minerals is not appropriate for drinking from a biological and medical point of view).
3. Drink water with a minimum of 50mg per liter dissolved Calcium and Magnesium.
4. Alkaline ionized water is more suitable than neutral or distilled water.

We need to take greater interest in the quality of water that we consume. In addition to quality food (proteins, carbohydrates, fats, vitamins, minerals, etc.), we need to understand that disease is also linked to the quality of the water we drink.

Water Contamination and Health

Since current research is beginning to show that water has memory, it becomes even more important for us to safeguard our water supplies. If water has the capacity to maintain the frequency of energies it is exposed to, then we must ask ourselves the question, "What are the consequences of drinking water that has been recycled from agricultural runoff, sewage plants, factories etc?"

Water contamination is emerging as a serious health issue - for more reasons than just the obvious. Vibrational contamination may be having even greater consequences than we have considered. Recycling water is similar to recycling paper. It must be processed with chemicals and bleaches in order to make it suitable for reuse. The biggest difference is that we do not *consume* recycled paper and it is not utilized in the function of nearly every bodily process.

It is time to re-evaluate our currents methods of water treatment. This may seem like a costly proposal, however, the long-term cost to our health may be even greater. A more conscientious effort to safeguard and preserve our water resources will result in considerable health benefits. Additionally, the use of Hexagonal Water will allow us to explore new levels of health and disease prevention.

**The use of Hexagonal Water
will allow us to explore new levels of health and
disease prevention.**

THE
WATER PUZZLE

Drinking Hexagonal Water

Chapter

6

THE WATER PUZZLE

Chapter 6
Drinking Hexagonal Water

Hexagonal Water for Health

Many scholars in the field of science and medicine are focusing on the relationship between water and life. In the field of medicine, health can actually be determined by the state of the water in and around the cells. More and more, doctors and scientists are coming to the conclusion that the quality of the water we drink plays a critical role in the quality of our health and that we can actually *improve* the quality of our health by improving the quality of the water we drink. In this regard, water has been determined to be an effective treatment for many illnesses. Not only is water related to the activities of life, but as we have seen, the structure of water actually plays a major role in many of these life-giving activities.

Hexagonal Water - comprised of small molecular units or ring-shaped clusters - moves easily within the cellular matrix of the body, helping with nutrient absorption and waste removal. It aids metabolic processes, supports the immune system, contributes to lasting vitality and acts as a carrier of dissolved oxygen. It can provide alkaline minerals to the body and it helps in the more efficient removal of acidic wastes. Drinking Hexagonal Water takes us in the direction of greater health. It supports long life and freedom from disease.

> **Hexagonal Water moves easily within the cellular matrix of the body, helping with nutrient absorption and waste removal.**

Biological Organisms Prefer Hexagonal Water

During the last 10 years, (the period of time when the role of structured water has been the most seriously investigated) it has been determined that human beings and other biological organisms prefer Hexagonal Water – that this specific structure both directly and indirectly supports biological functions. Several studies have been conducted, using melted snow, since it has the highest concentration of natural Hexagonal Water known. In one test, melted snow water was used to sprout wheat. Results showed that snow water was significantly more efficient at activating the enzymes released during sprouting. The dehydrogenase enzymes which are involved in the proton-motive force that drives the production of ATP (energy) were highly activated by melted snow water and the proton pumping mechanism was accelerated.

It is well known that proton transfer is accelerated in ice due to its structure. This is similar to the ease with which a baton can be handed off during a relay race if the runners are in close proximity during the transfer. Tightly held water molecules in ice and other structured solutions make proton transfers easy compared with less structured environments.

The above research concluded that the water from melted snow, encouraged proton pumping, which in turn activated the dehydrogenase enzymes for quicker sprouting. (See Table 7) Comparatively, Dioxane (a structure-breaking substance) disrupts the structure of water located near these enzymes causing a reduction in proton movement and a subsequent reduction in enzyme activity.

**Table 7. Water Structure and the Activation
of Dehydrogenase Enzymes**

Sample	Activation level	Relative value
Control	1,280 - 1,600	1
Snow water	1,558 - 1,600	1.04 - 1.30
Dioxane (4% DMF)	790 - 880	0.49 - 0.69

In a variety of similar research, Hexagonal snow water has produced the following results:

- An increase in crop harvests
- A proliferation of plant plankton
- Accelerated growth of Mudfish
- Accelerated chicken growth and increased egg-laying

There have even been reports claiming that a bat, frozen in ice near the North Pole, was resuscitated and lived. This makes sense if the water near the bat was in a super-cooled state (100% hexagonally structured). With such positive biological responses, we can no longer deny that Hexagonal Water is the water of choice for biological organisms – including the human body.

Hexagonal Water – the Best Water to Drink!

Even though the source of the water we drink is important, the structure of that water is the *key*. The best water for human consumption is Hexagonal Water. This water is characterized by a small cluster size (verified using NMR technology) which penetrates the cells much faster (verified with Bio Impedance testing), supplying nutrients and oxygen more efficiently than unstructured water. When Hexagonal Water replaces the unstructured water in the body, cell water turnover and cellular metabolism are enhanced - positively affecting many other functions.

In my opinion, the very best water to drink is melted snow from places like the Alps or the

Caucasus mountains. This melted snow water usually travels down mountains, gaining energy and oxygen and it has proven to be very good for all biological organisms. Unfortunately, most of us do not live in areas where this kind of structured and energized water is available and it is *not* advisable to drink snow water collected in cities where pollution is a problem. However, there are ways to create Hexagonal Water and energize it, even when we don't live in areas where snow water or other pristine water supplies exist. There are several commercial ventures that are already making Hexagonal Water available to the general public.

Creating Hexagonal Water

To make Hexagonal Water, the original water is better when it contains *structure-making* ions such as Calcium. Tap water with chlorine, fluoride and other chemicals does not satisfy the criteria for a good original water. Additionally, powerful energetic forces are required to make Hexagonal Water at room temperature. Both electric and magnetic fields are able to re-align the water molecules and overcome the need for freezing temperatures in the creation of Hexagonal Water. With this technology, Hexagonal Water can be made available for use in the medical field - for health maintenance and the treatment of disease. Magnetically processed water can be made available to the general public for daily consumption. It has been determined to be quite stable, with the ability to maintain its structure for extended periods of time.

Is Drinking Cold Water Better?

Many have asked about drinking *cold* water. Is it important to drink it cold? This is an interesting question. In light of our research, we know that cold water contains a higher percentage of hexagonal structures. We also know that as soon as cold water enters the body it is no longer cold. Does this affect the structure of the water?

Yes, it does. However, if you recall, we discussed that water has a kind of "memory." When consumed, Hexagonal Water temporarily changes into predominantly pentagonal water and the hexagonal structure is broken. But when water assumes its functions within a biological organism, it has the capacity to transform back to its original molecular structure. With this in mind, the most important consideration is whether or not the water was hexagonally structured *before* drinking. By using some form of structuring process, the water is energetically altered and preconditioned to hold the hexagonal form. This is ideal.

Beyond Theory

The study of Hexagonal Water has gone far beyond theory. It is now an accepted branch of science with commercial applications already in existence. In parts of the world, the production of Hexagonal Water is already providing benefits to the agricultural, industrial, animal and human markets and there are many other possibilities on the horizon. The medical and health industries stand to benefit greatly from this knowledge and the benefits to the frozen food industry go without saying.

In the Orient, the use of Hexagonal Water is well accepted and there is a great desire to consume it on a regular basis. Many have attempted to bring water from snowy mountains for consumption. Some have used expensive ionization generators or sought other methods to create Hexagonal Water for regular drinking. In the Orient, more than in the Western World, the theory that Hexagonal Water is important for our health has firmly established itself. We have found that Hexagonal Water is beneficial for the body, and that drinking pentagonal water can actually be harmful. If we are to live a long life, free of disease, we need to drink a sufficient amount of *Hexagonal Water* on a daily basis.

For a long time this information has been theory however, clinical research has begun to substantiate the theory and vast numbers of individuals are benefiting from the use of Hexagonal Water, today. Many of us who have been involved in this research wonder what kind of changes would take place if we could all drink water that was 100% hexagonally structured. It is an interesting thought to ponder.

Final Words

There is a saying in Korea, "We use water like we were using water." - similar to the expression, in English, "We use water like it was going out of style." In other words, we generally take little regard for this precious resource and as a result, much of our water is used and misused wastefully.

It is generally accepted that 60 - 70% of every living organism is water. However, there are scholars who claim that 90% of living organisms are water since only 10% remains when the water is evaporated. Whatever the case may be, water is the very foundation of our lives. It is an intrinsic part of everything we do and everything we are. Hopefully, an understanding of this can help us to be more grateful and to share in the responsibility to protect our water supplies.

For those who do not respect the natural flow of water, it can bring about calamities (drought and floods). And for those who forget to take care of natural water sources, it can bring about illnesses such as Typhus, Cholera, Dysentery and Enteritis. Only when we maintain quality water, can we become beneficiaries of its life-giving traits and escape the sickness it dispenses when we are not careful stewards.

The continual degradation of our water supplies on the planet creates serious health issues which may ultimately be the downfall of our existence. Fortunately, our awareness of the relationship between water and health is increasing and the desire to use water in an effective, resourceful manner is taking a greater priority. At this point, we are moving beyond the place where we have focused on the available *quantity* of water and we are in a position to understand and implement programs where we can focus on water *quality*.

Since water is the basis of life's activities, we cannot neglect it and expect to move forward with life and health. Thus far in our planetary existence, we have taken the value of water for granted, just like people in a family who take their family relationships for granted and forget matters of etiquette. Even our scientists, biologists and doctors have studied everything in water, without considering that the water itself and the *structure of the water* may be playing an equally, important role. Going forward, we have the opportunity to look at the whole picture and come to a more complete understanding of the relationship between water and life.

Until now, we have merely co-existed with water and it has largely controlled our destiny. At this point we are in a position take control. Careful management of the planet's water supply and the use of Hexagonal Water in our personal lives, can allow us greater freedom and abundant health as we move into the 21st century and beyond. This is my most humble desire.

Careful management of the planet's water supply and the use of Hexagonal Water in our personal lives, can allow us greater freedom and abundant health as we move into the 21st century and beyond.

111

THE
WATER PUZZLE

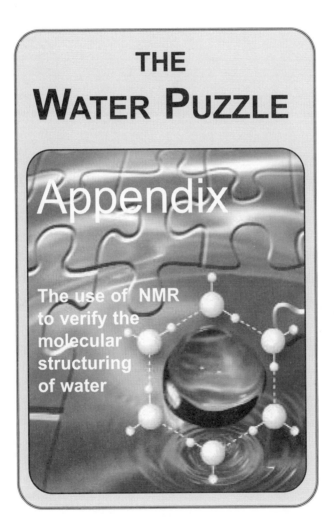

Appendix

The use of NMR
to verify the
molecular
structuring
of water

THE WATER PUZZLE

Appendix
The use of Nuclear Magnetic Resonance (NMR) to verify the molecular structuring of water

The application of pulsed NMR techniques in the area of biological systems is a valuable tool in helping to validate water structure. NMR relaxation times reflect the kinetic properties of water. Linewidth indicates the size of the molecular structure as determined by its rate of rotation.

The ^{17}O-NMR linewidth for normal tap water usually measures between 100 and 150 Hertz, indicating an unorganized state of the water and a cluster size of $(H_2O)_{12-13}$. Hexagonal Water usually measures between 60 and 70 Hz. - indicating a higher percentage of 6-ring structures $(H_2O)_6$.

The following table shows linewidths of tap water, magnetically-produced Hexagonal Water and several bottled water products obtained in Korea. It also shows the amount of dissolved oxygen in each sample.*

Water sample	^{17}O-NMR Linewidth (Hz.)	Dissolved Oxygen mg./l
Tap water	105.9	6.2
Magnetically-structured water	61.6	9.0
Bottled water - L	92.9	5.4
Bottled water - W	116.2	7.7
Bottled water - K	87.9	6.2

* *NMR test results - courtesy of Korea Basic Science Institute Dissolved Oxygen results - courtesy of Korea Testing & Research Institute.*

THE
WATER PUZZLE

About the Author

THE WATER PUZZLE

About the Author

Dr. Mu Shik Jhon was born in 1932 in Korea. As a young man, his love for the natural sciences took him to Seoul National University where he completed his undergraduate and graduate degrees in Chemistry. After 8 years as an assistant and associate professor at Dongguk University in Seoul, he decided to pursue a Ph.D. at the University of Utah under the direction of the famous Dr. Henry Eyring. As a result of their work together, he and Dr. Eyring became life-long friends. Between 1964 and 1982, they published nearly 50 scientific papers and one book together.

With the completion of his doctorate degree, Dr. Jhon accepted the position of assistant professor at the University of Virginia and then returned to Korea as head of the Liquid State Chemistry Research Laboratory at the Korea Institute of Science and Technology.

Between 1971 and 1974, Dr. Jhon served as a visiting professor with the University of Utah, where he is still an adjunct professor. He has also been a visiting professor at the University of Paris (1975-76), at Kyoto University in Japan (1980) and at the University of Florida (1986-87).

In 1971, Dr. Jhon became a professor of Chemistry at the Korea Advanced Institute of Science and Technology where he has been Dean of Faculty, Director of the Center for Molecular Science and Chair Professor.

During his career, Dr. MuShik Jhon has received upwards of 30 honors and awards, including the Grand Science Award and the Presidential Award of Science (the highest scientific award in Korea). He has spoken or presented papers at over 250 scientific gatherings and is recognized for his work on the Theory of Liquids, The Structure of Water, The Properties of Electrolyte Solutions, The Properties of the Hydrogen Bond, Statistical Mechanics, Chemical Rate Theory on Polymers and Quantum Chemistry.

Today, Dr. Jhon is still president or chairman of a number of scientific organizations and he is actively involved in academia – having published over 250 scientific papers in English, to date, with more in other languages.

Dr. Henry Eyring wrote in a letter commemorating Dr. Jhon's 50th birthday: "Of the 125 Ph.D's who have done their work with me, I would put none above Professor Jhon in ability and accomplishment. I think one could not find a better candidate for the highest academic post Korea has to offer."

Dr. Mu Shik Jhon is held in the highest esteem by his colleagues and associates and his dedication to the sciences and to all of mankind are evident in his life's work.

He has 3 children who are equally dedicated in their chosen professions – each with a PhD. Dr. Jhon lives in Seoul, Korea with his wife, Suk Won.

THE
WATER PUZZLE

Author's
Bibliography

Author's Bibliography

1. S. Chang, H. Pak, W. K. Paik, S. Park, M. S. Jhon and W. S. Ahn, Modified Theory of Significant Liquid Structure, *J. Korean Chem. Soc.* , **8**, 33 (1964).

2. M. S. Jhon and S. Chang, The Significant Structures of Liquid Fluorine, *J. Korean Chem. Soc.* , **8**, 65 (1964).

3. H. B. Lee, M. S. Jhon and S. Chang, Significant Structure of Liquid Ammonia, *J. Korean Chem. Soc.* , **8**, 179 (1964).

4. M. S. Jhon, J. Grosh, T. Ree and H. Eyring, The Significant Structure Theory Applied to meta- and para-Xylenes, *Proc. Natl. Acad. Sci.* , (U. S.), **54**. 1419 (1965).

5. J. Grosh, M. S. Jhon, T. Ree and H. Eyring, The Significant Structure Theory Applied to Liquid Hydrogen Halides, *Proc. Natl. Acad. Sci.* (U. S.), **54**, 1004 (1965).

6. M. S. Jhon, J. Grosh, T. Ree and H. Eyring, The Significant-Structure Theory Applied to Water and Heavy Water, *Abs. of the 149th An. Am. Chem. Soc. , Meeting (Detroit 1965). Abs. of the 16th AAAS Alaska Division Science Conference, Juneau, Alaska. J. Chem. Phys.* , **44**, 1465 (1966).

7. M. S. Jhon, J. Grosh, T. Ree and H. Eyring, The Significant Structure Theory Applied to the Hydrides of Elements of the Fifth Group, *J. Phys. Chem.* , **70**, 1591 (1966).

8. M. S. Jhon and S. W. Kim, Recent Development of Liquid Theory, *Progress in Chem. and Ind.* , **6**, 18 (1966). 9. H. Eyring and M. S. Jhon, The Significant Structure Theory of Water, *Chemistry*,**39**, No. 9, 8 (1966).

10. M. E. Hobbs, M. S. Jhon and H. Eyring, The Dielectric Constant of Liquid Water and Various Forms of Ice According to Significant Structure Theory, *Proc. Natl. Acad. Sci. (U. S.)*, **56**, 31 (1966).

11. M. S. Jhon and S. W. Kim, On the Dielectric Constants of Water and Various Forms of Ice According to Significant Structure Theory, *Progress in Chem. and Chemical Ind.* , **6**, 275 (1966).

12. M. E. Zandler and M. S. Jhon, Solutions of Nonelectrolytes, *Ann. Rev. Phys. Chem.* , 17, 373 (1966).

13. J. Grosh, M. S. Jhon, T. Ree and H. Eyring, Signifi-
cant Structure Theory of Isotope Effect, *Abs. of 151st Ann.
Am. Chem. Soc. , Meeting (Pittsburgh, 1966), Proc. Natl.
Acad. Sci. (U. S.)*, **58**, 2196 (1967).

14. M. S. Jhon, Comparison between Improved Onno's Free
Volume Approximation in Cell Theory and Significant Structure Theory of Liquid, *J. Korean Chem. Soc. *, **11**, 60 (1967).

15. M. S. Jhon, J. Grosh and H. Eyring, The Significant
Structure and Properties of Liquid Hydrazine and Liquid
Diborane, *J. Phys. Chem. *, **71**, 2253 (1967).

16. J. Grosh, M. S. Jhon, T. Ree and H. Eyring, On an
Improved Partition Function of Significant Structure Theory,
*Abs. 153rd Am. Chem. Soc. , Meeting (Miami, 1967), Proc.
Natl. Acad. Sci. (U. S.)*, **57**, 1566 (1967).

17. M. S. Jhon, E. R. Van Artsdalen, J. Grosh, and H.
Eyring, Further Applications of the Domain Theory of Liq-
uid Water: I. Surface Tension of Light and Heavy Water: II.
Dielectric Constant of Lower Aliphatic Alcohols, *Abs. of
153rd Am. Chem. Soc. , Meeting (Miami, 1967), J. Chem.
Phys. *, **47**, 2231 (1967).

18. W. C. Lu, M. S. Jhon, T. Ree and H. Eyring, Significant Structure Theory Applied to Surface Tension, *J. Chem.
Phys. *, **46**, 1075 (1967).

19. S. W. Kim, M. S. Jhon, T. Ree and H. Eyring, The
Surface Tension of Liquid Mixtures, *Proc. Natl. Acad. Sci.
(U. S.)*, **59**, 336 (1968). 20. M. S. Jhon, G. Clemena and E.
R. Van Artsdalen, The Significant Structures and Properties
of Molten Mercuric Halides, *J. Phys. Chem. *, **72**, 4155 (1968).

21. M. S. Jhon and H. Eyring, The Dielectric Constants of
Mixtures and of the Supercritical Region of Some H-Bonded
Fluids, *J. Am. Chem. Soc. (Debye Memorial Issue)*, **90**,
3071 (1968). 22. T. R. Schmidt, M. S. Jhon and H. Eyring,
The Significant Structure Theory Applied to Some Liquid
Rocket Fuels, *Proc. Natl. Acad. Sci. (U. S.)*, **60**, 387 (1968).

23. M. S. Jhon, The Significant Structure Theory of Dynamic Liquid Properties, *Abs. of Liquid Symposium, Cleve-
land, Ohio (1968, Nov.), New Physics, Korean Physical
Society*, **9**, 98 (1969).

24. M. S. Jhon and H. Eyring, An Improved Iteration Method for The Calculation of Surface Tension Using the Significant Structure Theory of Liquids, *Proc. Natl. Acad. Sci. (U. S.)*, **64**, 415 (1969).

25. M. S. Jhon, Sound Velocity and van der Waal's Force in Liquids, *J. Oceanological Soc. Korea*, **4**, 68 (1969).

26. M. S. Jhon, W. L. Klotz and H. Eyring, Theoretical Calculation of the Pressure Dependence of Liquid Hydrocarbon Viscosities, *Abs. of 155th Am. Chem. Soc. , Meeting (New York, 1969), J. Chem. Phys.* , **51**, 3692 (1969).

27. H. Eyring and M. S. Jhon, *Significant Liquid Structures, John Wiley & Sons, Inc. , New York* (1969).

28. T. Ree and M. S. Jhon, Derivation of the WLF Equation from the Theory of Rate Process, *J. Korean Chem. Soc.* , **14**, 45 (1970).

29. H. Eyring and M. S. Jhon, The Structure of Liquids: NASA Symposium, Interdisciplinary Approach to the Lubrication of Concentrated Contacts at RPI, N. Y. , (1969, July), Published by NASA (1970) pp. 249.

30. D. S. Choi and M. S. Jhon, The Significant Structure Theory on the Sound Velocity and Internal Pressure of Liquids, *Chem. Phys. Lett.* , **5**, 57 (1970).

31. Y. K. Sung and M. S. Jhon, Theoretical Calculations of Hydration Number and Activity Coefficients of Salts in Concentrated Electrolyte Solutions, *J. Korean Chem. Soc.* , **14**, 185 (1970).

32. J. S. Bahng, S. J. Hahn and M. S. Jhon, Liquid Viscosities of Binary Mixtures and Some Hydrocarbons in the High Pressure Range with Application of the Significant Structure Theory, *J. Korean Chem. Soc.* , **14**, 193 (1970).

33. D. S. Choi, M. S. Jhon and H. Eyring, Curvature Dependence of the Surface Tension and the Theory of Solubility, *J. Chem. Phys.* , **53**, 2608 (1970).

34. T. Kihara and M. S. Jhon, The Core Potential of Intermolecular Forces Applied to Solubility of Gases in Liquids, *Chem. Phys. Letter*, **7**, 559 (1970).

35. W. H. Paek, Y. K. Sung and M. S. Jhon, Surface Tension of Molten Salts and Strong Electrolyte Solution, *J. Korean Chem. Soc.* , **14**, 263 (1970).

36. Y. K. Sung and M. S. Jhon, On the Hydration Numbers and Activity Coefficients of Some Salts Present in Sea Water, *J. Oceanological Soc. Korea*, **5**, 1(1970).

37. B. K. Cho and M. S. Jhon, On the Reflection Coefficient in the Thermionic Emission, *J. Korean Institute of Metals*, **8**, 177 (1970).

38. T. Kihara, K. Yamazaki, M. S. Jhon and U. R. Kim, Core-Potential Parameters of Intermolecular Forces, *Chem. Phys. Letter*, **9**, 62 (1971).

39. M. S. Jhon and H. Eyring, The Significant Structure Theory of Liquids, *Advanced Treatise, Physical Chemistry, (Vol. 8), pp. 335 Academic Press* (1971).

40. J. S. Bahng, S. J. Hahn and M. S. Jhon, Viscosities of Supercooled Water and Other Liquids, *J. Korean Chem. Soc.* , **15**, 171 (1971).

41. U. R. Kim and M. S. Jhon, Fusion Mechanism of Liquid According to the Significant Liquid Structure Theory, *J. Korean Nuclear Society*, **3**, 33 (1971).   6

42. M. S. Jhon and S. K. Kim, The Theory of the One-Dimensional Lattice Defects, *J. Korean Chem. Soc.* , **15**, 165 (1971).

43. Y. K. Sung, U. H. Paek, and M. S. Jhon, Further Applications of the Solubility Theory to Various Systems, *J. Korean Chem. Soc.* , **15**, 211 (1971).

44. M. S. Jhon, Sound Velocity and van der Waal's Force in Liquids According to Significant Structure Theory, *Chemical Dynamics (John Wiley, 1971)* pp. 481.

45. M. S. Jhon, H. Eyring and Y. K. Sung, Solubility of Gases in Water, *Chem. Phys. Letter*, **13**, 36 (1971).

46. U. S. Kim, R. Schmidt, M. S. Jhon and H. Eyring, Physical Adsorption of Quantum Gas, *Proc. Natl. Acad. Sci. (U. S.)*, **69**, 1690 (1972). 47. W. S. Ahn, M. S. Jhon, H. Pak and S. Chang, Surface Tension of Curved Surfaces, *J. Colloid and Interface Sci.* , **38**, 605 (1972).

48. M. S. Jhon and U. I. Cho, Domain Structure of Liquid Water According to the Theory of Intermolecular Forces, *Abs. of 162nd Amer. Chem. Soc. Meeting (Washington D. C. , 1971), J. Korean Chem. Soc.* , **16**, 406 (1972).

49. M. S. Jhon, U. L. Cho, L. B. Kier and H. Eyring, Molecular Orbital Studies of Ethylenediamine Conformation, *Proc. Natl. Acad. Sci. (U. S.)*, **69**, 121 (1972).

50. M. S. Jhon, U. I. Cho, Y. B. Chae, and L. B. Kier, The Preferred Conformation of the Muscarinic Agent L(+) Acetyl-^{2}-Methylcholine, *J. Korean Chem. Soc.* ,**16**,70 (1972).

51. Y. K. Sung, U. S. Kim and M. S. Jhon, Thermodynamic Properties of Aliphatic and Aromatic Hydrocarbons in Liquid Water, *J. Korean Chem. Soc.* , **16**, 413 (1972).

52. Y. B. Chae, U. I. Cho and M. S. Jhon, Molecular Orbital Consideration of the Conformation of Chloramphenicol, *J. Korean Chem. Soc.* , **16**, 419 (1972).

53. Y. U. Park, M. S. Jhon and J. W. Kim, The Study on Ni-Cd Cell, *J. Korean Chem. Soc.* , **15**, 347 (1973).

54. M. S. Jhon and J. Andrade, Water and Hydrogels, *J. Biomedical Materials Research*, **7**, 509 (1973).

55. U. R. Kim, M. S. Jhon and Y. B. Chae, Sweet Taste Mechanism of 1-Alkoxy-4- nitroaniline, *J. Korean Chem. Soc.* , **17**, 438 (1973).

56. J. D. Andrade, H. B. Lee, M. S. Jhon, S. W. Kim and J. B. Hibbs, Water as a Biomaterial, *Trans. Amer. Soc. Art. Int. Org.* , 1 (1973).

57. S. W. Kim and M. S. Jhon, Polymer Membranes, Its Application to Artificial Kidney, *Progress in Chem. and Ind. (Korean Chem. Soc.)*, **13**, 271 (1973).

58. S. M. Ma, H. Eyring and M. S. Jhon, The Significant Structure Theory Applied to Amorphous and Crystalline Polyethylene, *Proc. Natl. Acad. Sci. (U. S.)*, **71**, 3096 (1974).

59. U. R. Kim, M. S. Jhon, U. S. Kim and Y. B. Chae, The Synthesis, NMR Sepectrum and Molecular Orbital Theoretical Studies on MBBA and EBBA, *J. Korean Chem. Soc.* , **18**, 453 (1974).

60. H. B. Lee, J. D. Andrade and M. S. Jhon, Nature of Water in Synthetic Gels II, Proton Pulse NMR of

Polyhydroxyethyl Methacrylate, *Polymer Preprint*, **15**, 391 (1974).

61. H. B. Lee, M. S. Jhon and J. D. Andrade, Nature of Water in Synthetic Hydrogels I. Dilatometry Specific Conductivity and Differential Scanning Calorimetry of Polyhydroxyethyl Methacrylate, *J. Colloid and Interface Sci.* , **51**, 225 (1975).

62. M. S. Jhon, Nature of Water in Synthetic Hydrogel, *Proceeding of Center for Theoretical Physics and Chemistry, Seoul, Korea (1975)* pp. 99.

63. U. S. Kim, Y. K. Sung, M. S. Jhon and H. Eyring, Physical Adsorption of Some Hydrocarbons, The Two Dimensional Liquid State, *Physics and Chemistry of Liquid,* **1,** 61 (1976).

64. M. S. Jhon, H. B. Lee, S. W. Kim and J. D. Andrade, Ion Permeability, Dehydration and Relaxation Times of Hydrated Ions Through Membranes, *J. Korean Chem. Soc.* , **20**, 424 (1976).

65. M. S. Jhon, S. M. Ma, S. Hattori, D. E. Gregonis and J. D. Andrade, The Role of Water in the Osmotic and Viscoelastic Behavior of Gel Networks, Amer. Chem. Soc. Symposia (Chicago, 1975), *Polymer Preprint 16, 281 (1975), ACS Symposium Series 31, pp. 60 (1975) (American Chemical Society).*

66. M. S. Jhon and H. Eyring, Liquid Theory and the Structure of Water, *Ann. Rev. Phys. Chem.* , **27**, 45 (1976).

67. Y. Do, M. S. Jhon and T. Ree, Theoretical Prediction of the Thermodynamic Properties of Liquid-Crystalline p-Azoxyanisole, *J. Korean Chem. Soc.* , **20**, 379 (1976).

68. Y. Oh and M. S. Jhon, Isotope Effects on Vapor Pressure, *J. Korean Chem. Soc. ,* **21**, 75 (1977).

69. S. H. Lee, M. S. Jhon and H. Eyring, Significant Structure Theory Applied to Phase Separation, *Proc. Natl. Acad. Sci. (U. S.),* **74**, 10 (1977).

70. S. Choi, M. S. Jhon and J. D. Andrade, Nature of Water in Synthetic Hydrogels III, Dilatometry, Specific Conductiv-

ity, and Dielectric Relaxation of PGMA, *J. Colloid and Interface Sci.* , **61**, 1 (1977).

71. D. W. Moon, M. S. Jhon and T. Ree, Theoretical Calculation of Activity Coefficients of Liquid Mixtures, *J. Korean Chem. Soc.* , **21**, 395 (1977).

72. D. Perahia, M. S. Jhon and B. Pullman, Theoretical Study of the Hydration of B-DNA, *Biochimica Biophysica Acta*, **474**, 349 (1977).

73. Y. Oh, M. S. Jhon and H. Eyring, Significant Structure Theory Applied to Liquid Helium Three, *Proc. Natl. Acad. Sci. (U. S.)*, **74**, 4739 (1977).

74. K. H. Lee, J. G. Jee, M. S. Jhon and T. Ree, Solute Transport Through Crosslinked Poly(2-Hydroxyethyl Methacrylate) Membrane, *J. of Bioengineering,* **2**, 269 (1978).

75. M. S. Jhon and H. Eyring, A Model of the Liquid State, Three Phase Partition Functions, *Theoretical Chemistry, Academic Press,* 1978. 76. J. M. Lee and M. S. Jhon, Theoretical Study of the Hydration of Collagen, *J. Korean Chem. Soc.* , **22**, 403 (1978).

77. J. G. Jee, M. S. Jhon and T. Ree, Transport of Some Solutes in Blood Plasma Through poly(2-Hydroxyethyl Methacrylate) Hydrogel Membrane, *J. Korean Chem. Soc.* , **22**, 304 (1978).

78. K. Kim and M. S. Jhon, Theoretical Study of Hydration of RNA, *Biochimica Biophysica Acta*, **565**, 131 (1979).

79. K. T. No, and M. S. Jhon, Theoretical Study of Hydration of Zeolite NaA, *J. Korean Chem. Soc.* , **23**, 374 (1979).

80. Y. Oh, J. D. Andrade and M. S. Jhon, Theoretical Estimation of Interfacial Tension between Molten Polymers, *J. Korean Chem. Soc.* , **23**, 210 (1979).

81. J. M. Lee, M. S. Jhon and H. Eyring, Significant Structure Theory Applied to Electrolyte Solution, *Proc. Natl. Acad. Sci. (U. S.)*, **76**, 5421 (1979).

82. Y. Oh and M. S. Jhon, Theoretical Estimation of Surface Tension of Amorphous High Polymer, *J. Colloid and Interface Sci.* , **73**, 467 (1980).

83. R. Ryoo, M. S. Jhon and H. Eyring, Significant Structure Theory Applied to Liquid Helium Four, *Proc. Natl. Acad. Sci. (U. S.)*, **77**, 18 (1980).

84. H. S. Koo and M. S. Jhon, The Transport Phenomena of a Series of Amides Through the Copolymer Hydrogel Membranes, *Bull. Korean Chem. Soc.* , **1**, 138 (1980).

85. J. M. Lee and M. S. Jhon, The Significant Structure Theory of Liquids Applied to Homogeneous Nucleation Theory, *Bull. Korean Chem. Soc.* , **1**, 26 (1980).

86. R. Ryoo, M. S. Jhon and H. Eyring, Temperature and Pressure Dependence of Viscosity of Quantum Liquid 4He According to Significant Structure Theory, *Proc. Natl. Acad. Sci. (U. S.)*, **77**, 4399 (1980).

87. M. S. Jhon, Models in Research, *Proc. of 7th U. S. - Korean Scientists and Engineering Symposia (Seoul, Korea) pp. 209-215 (1980).*

88. H. Eyring, M. S. Jhon and T. Ree, Reaction Rates Including Fast Reactions in Energetic Systems, *Fast Reactions in Energetic Systems, pp. 47-54, D. Reidel Pub. Co. (1981).*

89. Y. K. Kang and M. S. Jhon, Theoretical Study of Isotope and Cation Binding Effects on the Hydration of B-DNA, *Bull. Korean Chem. Soc.* , **2**, 24 (1981).

90. K. O. Koh and M. S. Jhon, Theoretical Study of Effects of Cation on t-RNA, *Bull. Korean Chem. Soc.* , **2**, 66 (1981).

91. E. H. Kim, S. I. Jeon, S. C. Yoon and M. S. Jhon, The Nature of Water in Tactic Poly (2-Hydroxyethyl Methacrylate) Hydrogels, *Bull. Korean Chem. Soc.* , **2**, 60 (1981).

92. J. M. Lee and M. S. Jhon, Application of Liquid Theory to Sodium-Ammonia Solution, *Bull. Korean Chem. Soc.* , **2**, 90 (1981).

93. K. T. No, H. Chon, T. Ree and M. S. Jhon, Theoretical Studies on Acidity and Site Selectivity of Cations in Faujasite Zeolite, *J. Phys. Chem.* , **85**, 2065 (1981).

94. Y. K. Kang and M. S. Jhon, A New Empirical Potential Function and Its Application to Hydrogen Bonding, *Bull. Korean Chem. Soc.* , **2**, 8 (1981).

95. B. J. Yoon, M. S. Jhon and H. Eyring, Radial Distribution Function of Liquid Argon According to Significant Structure Theory, *Proc. Natl. Acad. Sci. (U. S.)*, **78**, 6588 (1981).

96. Y. K. Sung, M. S. Jhon, D. E. Gregonis and J. D. Andrade, Thermal and Pulse NMR Analysis of Water in P(HEMA), *J. Appl. Poly. Sci.* , **26**, 3719 (1981).

97. H. G. Cho, S. C. Yoon and M. S. Jhon, The Reduced Equation of State and Related Properties of Molten High Polymers, *J. Poly. Sci.* . **20**, 1247 (1982).

98. J. G. Jee, O. C. Kwun, M. S. Jhon and T. Ree, A Study for the Viscous Flow of Sodium Chloride Through a Cuprophane Membrane, *Bull. Korean Chem. Soc.* , **3**, 23 (1982).

99. Y. K. Kang and M. S. Jhon, Additivity of Atomic Static Polarizabilities and Dispersion Coefficients, *Theoret. Chim. Acta,* **61**, 41 (1982).

100. H. Y. Park and M. S. Jhon, Thermodynamic and Transport Properties of Liquid Gallium, *J. Korean Nuc. Soc.* , **14**, 10 (1982).

101. S. C. Yoon and M. S. Jhon, The Transport Phenomena of Some Model Solutes through Postcrosslinked Poly(2-Hydroxylethyl Methacrylate) Membranes with Different Tacticity, *J. Applied Polym. Sci.* , **27**, 3133 (1982).

102. S. C. Yoon and^ M. S. Jhon,^ Temperature Effect on the Permeation through P(HEMA) Membrane Transport, *J. Appl. Poly. Sci.* , **27**, 4661 (1982).

103. M. C. Chang and M. S. Jhon, Viscosity and Thermodynamic Properties of Liquid Sulfur, *Bull. Korean Chem. Soc.* , **3**, 133 (1982).

104. Y. J. Park, Y. K. Kang, B. S. Yoon and M. S. Jhon, Theoretical Study on Structure and Energetics of Small Water Clusters, *Bull. Korean Chem. Soc.* , **3**, 50 (1982).

105. M. S. Jhon, The Improved Significant Structure Theory Applied to Water and Heavy Water, *Memorial Issue of Song Jung, Sam Ill Cultural Foundation,* 1982.

106. K. T. No and M. S. Jhon, M. O. Calculation of Several Ices Using the Pseudolattice Method, *J. Phys. Chem.*, **87**, 226 (1983).

107. M. S. Jhon and B. J. Yoon, An Extended Significant Structure Theory Applied to Water and Heavy Water, *Ions and Molecules in Solutions, Elsevier Sci. Pub. Corp.*, (1983), **27**, pp. 29-44.

108. J. W. Lee, E. H. Kim and M. S. Jhon, The Swelling and Mechanical Properties of Hydrogels of Tactic p(HEMA), *Bull. Korean Chem. Soc.*, **4**, 162 (1983).

109. H. K. Kim and M. S. Jhon, Self Diffusion of THO within Tactic p-HEMA Membranes, *Bull. Korean Chem. Soc.*, **4**, 128 (1983).

110. E. H. Kim, S. I. Jeon, B. Y. Moon and M. S. Jhon, The Nature of Water in Copolymer Hydrogels, *Bull. Korean Chem. Soc.*, **4**, 251 (1983).

111. M. J. Moon, Y. K. Kang and M. S. Jhon, Conformational Study of Y-Base in Yeast t-RNAphe, *Bull. Korean Chem. Soc.*, **4**, 133 (1983).

112. M. S. Jhon, Graduate Education and Scientific Creativity, *J. of Chem. Educ.*, Korea, 110 (1983).

113. M. S. Jhon, Water, *Science*, No. 12 (1983).

114. Y. K. Sung, M. S. Jhon, D. E. Gregonis and J. D. Andrade, Water Vapor Sorption of Stereoregular Poly(2-Hydroxyethyl Methacrylate) and Poly (2,3-Dihydroxypropyl Methacrylate) *Polymer*, **8**, 123 (1984).

115. C. N. Yoon, Y. K. Kang and M. S. Jhon, Conformational Study of Trinucleoside Tetraphosphate d(pCpGpCp): Transition of Right-Handed Form to Left-Handed Form, *Biopolymer*, **23**, 511 (1984).

116. Y. K. Kang and M. S. Jhon, Conformational Study of the Dinucleotide dGpdCp-Tetrapeptide Ala4 Complex, *Macromolecules*, **17**, 138 (1984).

117. J. S. Kim, K. T. No and M. S. Jhon, Further Applications of Molecular Orbital Caclulations for Solid HF According to Pseudolattice Method, *Bull. Korean Chem. Soc.*, **5**, 61 (1984).

118. H. Y. Jung and M. S. Jhon, Partial Miscibility in Multicomponent Polymer System, *J. Poly. Sci.*, **22**, 567 (1984).

119. B. J. Yoon and M. S. Jhon, The Anomalies of Supercooled Water, *Bull. Korean Chem. Soc.*, **5**, 82 (1984).

120. H. Y. Jung and M. S. Jhon, Partial Miscibility in Water-Nicotine and Water-^{2}-Picolin System, Bull. *Korean Chem. Eng. Soc.*, **1**, 59 (1984).

121. S. H. Oh, M. C. Jhang and M. S. Jhon, Molecular Orbital Calculation for Polymeric Beryllium Hydride, Polyethylene and Polymeric Boron Hydride According to the Pseudo-Lattice Method, *Bull. Korean Chem. Soc.*, **5**, 37 (1984).

122. S. J. Choe, U. S. Kim, Y. K. Kang and M. S. Jhon, Theoretical Study of the Hydration Effects on the Conformations of N-Pivaloyl-L-Prolyl-N-Methyl-N'-Isopropyl-L-Alaninamide, *Bull. Korean Chem. Soc.*, **5**, 27 (1984).

123. S. I. Jeon and M. S. Jhon, Dilute Solution Properties of Tactic Poly(2-Hydroxyethyl Methacrylate), *J. Poly. Sci.*, **22**, 3555 (1984).

124. S. H. Yuk, S. I. Jeon and M. S. Jhon, Temperature Dependence of Self-Diffusion of THO in Copolymer Hydrogel Membrane as a Function of Gel Compositions, *Bull. Korean Chem. Soc.*, **5**, 104 (1984).

125. E. H. Lee, S. I. Jeon and M. S. Jhon, Some Model Solute Affinity for a Tactic P(HEMA) Membranes by KD Measurement, *Bull. Korean Chem. Soc.*, **5**, 175 (1984).

126. M. S. Jhon and Y. Oh, Interfacial Tensions at Amorphous High Polymers-Water Interfaces: Theory, Surface and Interfacial Aspects of Biomedical Polymers, Vol. 1, Surface Chemistry and Physics, Plenum Press (1985) pp 395-420.

127. M. C. Chang, R. Ryoo and M. S. Jhon, Thermodynamic Properties of Liquid Carbon, *Carbon*, **23**, 418 (1985).

128. K. O. Koh and M. S. Jhon, Theoretical Study of Ionic Selectivities and Adsorption of Water in Zeolite A, *Zeolites*, **5**, 313 (1985).

129. M. C. Chang, H. Y. Kim and M. S. Jhon, Vibrational Assignment of S8 from a Normal Coordinate Analysis, *Bull. Korean Chem. Soc.*, **6**, 29 (1985).

130. H. Y. Jung and M. S. Jhon, Theoretical Estimations of Partial Miscibilities by the Extended Flory-Huggins Lattice Theory, *Bull. Korean Chem. Soc.* , **6**, 132 (1985).

131. M. C. Chang and M. S. Jhon, Normal Mode Studies of Solids HF, HCl and Polyethylene According to the Pseudolattice Method, *Bull. Korean Chem. Soc.* , **6**, 57,(1985).

132. K. T. No and M. S. Jhon, Lattice Vibrational Calculation of Orthorhombic Hydrogen Chloride, *Bull. Korean Chem. Soc.* , **6**, 183 (1985).

133. Y. S. Kong, K. T. No and M. S. Jhon, Normal Mode Calculation of Faujasite-Type Zeolite Frameworks, *Bull. Korean Chem. Soc.* , **6**, 57 (1985).

134. W. G. Kim and M. S. Jhon, The Transport Phenomena of Some Solute Through the Copolymer Membranes of 2-Hydroxyethylmethacrylate (HEMA) with Selected Hydrophobic Monomers, *Bull. Korean Chem. Soc.* , **6**, 128 (1985).

135. C. N. Yoon and M. S. Jhon, Intermediate Water Structures in Solution of Alanine Dipeptide, *Int. J. Quantum Chem.* , **12**, 33 (1986).

136. C. N. Yoon and M. S. Jhon, Conformational Study of the Trinucleotide CpGpCp- Pentapeptide Gly5 Complex; The Important Role of Bridging Water in the Complex Formation, *J. Computational Chem.* , **7**, 189 (1986).

137. D. H. Bae, K. T. No and M. S. Jhon, Lattice Vibrational Calculation of A-type Zeolite Using Pseudolattice Method, *J. Phys. Chem.* , **90**, 1772 (1986).

138. K. H. Koh, H. Chon and M. S. Jhon, Site Selectivity of Alkaline Earth Metal Cations in Zeolite A, *J. Catalysis,* **98**, 126 (1986).

139. S. H. Yuk and M. S. Jhon, Contact Angles on Deformable Solids, *J. Colloid and Interface Sci.* , **110**, 252 (1986).

140. M. J. Moon and M. S. Jhon, The Studies of Hydration Energy and Water Structures in Dilute Aqueous Solution, *Bull. Japan Chem. Soc.* , **59**, 1215 (1986).

141. B. J. Yoon and M. S. Jhon, Phase Transition and Approximated Integral Equation for Radial Distribution Function, *Bull. Korean Chem. Soc.* , **7**, 20 (1986).

142. D. H. Baik, B. J. Yoon and M. S. Jhon, The Calculation of Hugoniot Adiabatics and Viscosity of Shock Compressed Water, *Bull. Korean Chem. Soc.*, **7**, 293 (1986).

143. Y. S. Kong and M. S. Jhon, Solvent Effect on SN 2 Reactions, *Theor. Chimica Acta*, **70**, 123 (1986).

144. D. H. Baik, Y. S. Lee and M. S. Jhon, Ab Initio SCF Calculations of the Linear Infinite Chain of LiH According to the Pseudo-Lattice Method, *Theor. Chimica Acta*, **70**, 227 (1986).

145. S. D. Hong and M. S. Jhon, Theoretical Study on the Role of Water in Anesthesia, *Bull. Korean Chem. Soc.*, **7**, 388 (1986).

146. S. H. Yuk and M. S. Jhon, Temperature Dependence of the Contact Angle at the Polymer-Water Interface, *J. Colloid Interface Sci.*, **116**, 25 (1987).

147. M. J. Moon, Y. K. Kang and M. S. Jhon, Effect of Hydration and Metal Ions on the Conformation of Daunomycin, *Bull. Korean Chem. Soc.*, **8**, 39 (1987).

148. K. T. No, J. S. Kim, Y. Y. Huh, W. K. Kim and M. S. Jhon, Intraframework Potential Energy Function of Zeolites 1. (T2O4Na)n-Type Na-A Zeolite, *J. Phys. Chem.*, **91**, 740 (1987).

149. M. S. Jhon and S. H. Yuk, Contact Angles on Polymer-Water Surface; Temperature Dependence and Induced Deformation, in *"Polymer Surface Dynamics", Plenum Press (1987)*.

150. W. G. Kim, S. I. Jeon and M. S. Jhon, Conformational Properties of Isotactic poly(2-Hydroxyethyl Methacrylate) in the Mixed Water-Alcohol Solvents, *J. Poly. Sci.*, **25**, 467 (1987).

151. J. M. Shin, F. Toda and M. S. Jhon, Studies on Hydroxy Inclusion Complexes. 1. Host-Guest Interaction of the Molecular Complexes of 9-Hydroxy-9-(1-propynyl) fluorene and 1,1-Bis(2,4-dimethylphenyl)-2-butyn-1-ol with Water, Methanol, Ethanol, and n-Propanol, *J. Inclusion Phenomena*, **5**, 567 (1987).

152. M. S. Jhon, J. M. Shin and F. Toda, Theoretical Studies of Relative Stabilities of Guest Molecules in Hydroxy Host Inclusion Complexes (Host Guest Interaction of Mo-

lecular Complexes of 9-Hydroxy-9-(1-Propynyl) Fluorene and 1,1-Bis(2,4-Dimethyl)-1-Butyn-1-ol with Water, Methanol, Ethanol, and n-Propanol), *Physical Organic Chemistry, Elsevier, Amsterdam*, **31**, 545 (1987).

153. K. J. Choi, K. T. No and M. S. Jhon, Theoretical Studies on Aluminophosphate-5 (AlPO4-5), *Bull. Korean Chem. Soc.* , **8**, 155 (1987).

154. M. K. Kim, S. H. Yuk and M. S. Jhon, Surface Interfacial Energetic Analysis of Amphiphilic Copolymer, *Bull. Korean Chem. Soc.* , **8**, 158 (1987).

155. M. S. Jhon, Water Environment Theory and Modern Diseases, *Proc. 10th U. S. -Korea Scientists and Engineering Symposia (Inchon, Korea), (1987)*

156. M. S. Jhon, Water as Diseases and Agings, *Proc. Water Utilization Res. Soc. Japan, (1988)*.

157. Y. S. Kong, M. S. Jhon and P. O. Lowdin, Studies on Proton Transfers in Water Clusters and DNA Base Pairs, *Int. J. Quantum Chem.* , **14**, 189 (1987).

158. M. S. Jhon, Physico-chemical Approaches to the Role of Water in Modern Diseases such as Cancer, Diabetes and AIDS, *Speculations in Science and Technology,* **10**, 179 (1987).

159. M. S. Jhon and P. O. Lowdin, Some Remarks on Certain Magnetic Properties of Water in the Study of Cancer, *Int. J. Quantum Chem.* , **14**, 9 (1987).

160. S. Kim, C. N. Yoon and M. S. Jhon, Intermediate Water Structures in Solution of ±- Acetyl-N-methylphenylalaninamide, *J. Comp. Chem.* , **9**, 125 (1988).

161. W. G. Kim and M. S. Jhon, Participation of Water in Conformational Change of Isotactic PHEMA as Studied by Viscometry in Various Electrolytic Solutions, *J. Poly. Sci.* , **26**, 859 (1988).

162. M. Y. Song, S. Kim and M. S. Jhon, A Theoretical Study on the Hydration of B-and Z-DNA Double Helices, *J. Molec. Structure*, **179**, 427 (1988).

163. D. H. Baik and M. S. Jhon, Ab Initio Studies of Lithium Bonded Complexes with H2O Molecule, *Bull. Korean Chem. Soc.* , **9**, 126 (1988).

164. J. M. Shin, K. T. No and M. S. Jhon, MD Study on the Na Ions Bound in A-type Zeolite Framework, *J. Phys. Chem.* , **92**, 4533 (1988).

165. U. H. Paek, M. C. Suh, Y. K. Sung and M. S. Jhon, Internal Pressure of Polymers, *Proc. MACRO 88, IUPAC (Kyoto, Japan).*

166. M. K. Song, H. Chon, K. T. No and M. S. Jhon, A Theoretical Study of the Stability of Ba-Exchanged Na-A Type Zeolites, *J. Molec. Catalysis,* **47**, 73 (1988).

167. K. T. No, B. H. Seo, J. M. Park and M. S. Jhon, Lattice Vibrational Calculation of A-type Zeolite, *J. Phys. Chem.* , **92**, 6783 (1988).

168. T. S. Chair, W. Kim, H. Pak and M. S. Jhon, A Calculation for the Viscosity of Fluid by Using van der Waals Equation of State, *Korean J. Chem. Eng.* , **92**, 7216 (1988).

169. S. Kim, M. S. Jhon and H. A. Scheraga, Analytic Intermolecular Potential Functions from Ab Initio SCF Calculations of Interaction Energies between CH4, CH3OH, CH3COOH, and CH3COO- and Water, *J. Phys. Chem.* , **92**, 7216 (1988).

170. M. S. Jhon, Molecular Theory of Water Enironment, *Science*, No. 12, (1988).

171. S. I. Jeon and M. S. Jhon, Effect of Ureas on the Viscometric Behavior of Water-Soluble Isotactic p(HEMA), *J. Poly. Sci.* , **27**, 237 (1989).

172. G. Y. Kweon, J. M. Shin, F. Toda and M. S. Jhon, Theoretical Study of the Inclusion Properties of 1,2,4,5-Tetra(morpholinocarbonyl)-benzene, *J.Inclusion Phenomena,* **7**, 363 (1989).

173. K. T. No, Y. Y. Huh and M. S. Jhon, Intraframework Potential Energy Function of Zeolites. 2. (SiAlO4Na)n Type NaA Zeolite, *J. Phys. Chem.* , **93**, 6413 (1989).

174. K. T. No, J. S. Kim and M. S. Jhon, Intraframework Potential Energy Function of Zeolites, *Theor. Chimica Acta*, **75**, 461 (1989).

175. K. T. No, B. H. Seo and M. S. Jhon, Normal Mode Calculation and IR Band Assignments of A-type Zeolite, *Theor. Chimica Acta*, **75**, 307 (1989).

176. M. S. Jhon, Role of Water as Our Life Expectancy due to the Agings and Various Cancers, *Bull. Korean Chem. Soc.*, **10**, 206 (1989).

177. S. H. Oh, R. Ryoo and M. S. Jhon, Molecular Motions of Tactic p-HEMA in Solutions Studied by 13C-NMR Relaxation Measurements, *J. Poly. Chem.*, **27**, 1383 (1989).

178. S. H. Oh and M. S. Jhon, Temperature Dependence of Unperturbed Dimensions for Isotactic p(HEMA), *J. Poly. Sci.*, **27**, 1731 (1989).

179. M. K. Song, J. M. Shin, H. Chon and M. S. Jhon, Molecular Dynamics Study on the Collapse of A-type Zeolite Framework. 1. Temperature Dependence and Prediction of Melting Phenomena, *J. Phys. Chem.*, **93**, 6463 (1989).

180. Y. S. Kong and M. S. Jhon, Theoretical Studies on the Potential Energy Profiles for Proton Transfer Reaction in Formamide Dimer, *Bull. Korean Chem. Soc.*, **10**, 488 (1989).

181. S. S. Wee, S. M. Kim and M. S. Jhon, Analytical Intermolecular Potential Function from ab Initio SCF Calculations for Hydration of Methylamine and Methylammonium Ion, *J. Phys. Chem.*, **94**, 1656 (1990).

182. B. J. Yoon, M. S. Jhon and H. A. Scheraga, Vibrational Quantum Correction for the L-J Fluid ; A Formalism of Effective Intermolecular Potentials Depending on Mass and Temperature, *J. Chem. Phys.*, **92**, 3748 (1990).

183. S. H. Oh, R. Ryoo and M. S. Jhon, Iodine-127 and Potassium-39 NMR Study of the Interaction of Ions with Water-Soluble Polymers, *Macromolecules*, **23**, 1671 (1990).

184. K. T. No, M. S. Jhon and H. A. Scheraga, Determination of Net Atomic Charges Using a Revised PEOE Method 2. Application to Ionic and Conjugated Molecules as Models for Polypeptides, *J. Phys. Chem.*, **94**, 4740 (1990).

185. M. K. Song, H. Chon and M. S. Jhon, MD Study on the Collapse of A-Type Zeolite Framework, 2. Prediction of the Structural Transformation by Fitting the RDF, *J. Phys. Chem.*, **94**, 7671 (1990).

186. M. Y. Song and M. S. Jhon, MC Simulation on the Hydration of Vitamin C Molecules, *J. Molec. Liq.* , **47**, 35 (1990).

187. I. H. Roe, K. W. Choi and M. S. Jhon, Therapeutic Effect of the Alkaline Ionized Water in the Patients with Chronic Idiopathic Constipation, *Korean J. of Gastroentelogy*, **22**, 802 (1990).

188. S. K. Kang and M. S. Jhon, Morphology and Surface Properties of Block Copolymers of P(±-methylstyrene) and P(2-hydroxyethyl methacrylate), *J. Colloid and Interface Sci.* , **144**, 390 (1991).

189. Y. S. Kong and M. S. Jhon, Ab Initio SCF Calculations of Potential Energy Surfaces for the Proton Transfer in a Formamide Dimer, *Bull. Korean Chem. Soc.* , **12**, 22 (1991).

190. J. H. Yoon, J. M. Shin, Y. K. Kang and M. S. Jhon, Conformational Analysis of p(HEMA), *J. Poly. Chem.* , **29**, 393 (1991).

191. Y. S. Kong and M. S. Jhon, External Ion Effects on Proton Transfer in the Formamide Dimer, *Bull. Korean Chem. Soc.* , **12**, 483 (1991).

192. J. K. Shin and M. S. Jhon, HDMC Procedure Coupled with the Temperature Heating and Annealing; As a Method to Obtain the Global Energy Minimum Structure of Polypeptides & Proteins, *Biopolymer*, **31**, 177 (1991).

193. B. J. Yoon, S. D. Hong, M. S. Jhon and H. A. Scheraga, Calculation of the Entropy and the Chemical Potential from RFSDF, *Chem. Phys. Lett.* , **181**, 73, (1991)

194. J. D. Song, R. Ryoo and M. S. Jhon, Anion Binding Properties of Poly(vinylpyrolidone) in Aqueous Solution Studied by Halide NMR Spectroscopy, *Macromolecules*, **24**, 1727 (1991).

195. G. Y. Kweon, H. A. Scheraga, and M. S. Jhon, Monte Carlo Treatment of Models for Side Chains of Proteins, *J. Phys. Chem.* , **95**, 8964 (1991)

196. B. J. Yoon, and M. S. Jhon, Ab initio Potential Function of Flexible Water-Water Interaction, *Chem. Phys. Lett.* , **178**, 253 (1991).

197. B. J. Yoon, and M. S. Jhon, Stability of Pentagon Structure of Water Cluster, *Bull. Korean. Chem. Soc.*, **12**, 67 (1991).

198. J. Y. Yu and M. S. Jhon, MD Study on the Properties of Water Clusters, *J. Colloid and Interface Sci.*, **147**, 443 (1991).

199. Y. K. Kang and M. S. Jhon, Free Energy and Hydration Free Energy of Ac-Ala-NHMe, *Bull. Korean Chem. Soc.*, **12**, 495 (1991).

200. J. S. Lee, M. K. Song and M. S. Jhon, MD Study on the Structural Phase Transition of Crystalline AgI, *Bull. Korean Chem. Soc.*, **12**, 490 (1991).

201. M. Y. Song and M. S. Jhon, MD Study of the Effect of Ion Concentration on the B-, Z-DNA and DNA-Daunomycin Complex, *J. Molec. Struc.*, **257**, 33 (1992)

202. S. D. Hong, B. J. Yoon and M. S. Jhon, Calculations of Excess Free Energy from Averaged Effective Acceptance Ratio in Monte Carlo Simulation for Argon, Nitrogen and Water, *Chem. Phys. Lett.*, **188**, 299 (1992).

203. S. D. Hong, B. J. Yoon and M. S. Jhon, Calculation of Excess Free Energy from Averaged Acceptance Ratio in MC Simulation for Hard Sphere and Hard Dumbell Fluids, *Molec. Phys.*, **75**, 355, (1992)

204. J. H. Yang, J. K. Shin and M. S. Jhon, The Structural Variation and Probability Redistribution in Alanine Dipeptide Conformers by the Hydration, *J. Molec. Struc.*, **268**, 169 (1992)

205. J. H. Lee, H. G. Kim, G. S. Hang, H. B. Lee and M. S. Jhon, Characterization of Wettability Gradient Surfaces Prepared by Corona Discharge Treatment, *J. Colloid Interface Sci.*, **151**, 563 (1992)

206. B. J. Yoon, M. S. Jhon and H. A. Scheraga, MC Simulation of the Hard-Sphere Fluid with High-Temperature Quantum Correction in the Region of Fluid-Solid Phase Transition, *J. Chem. Phys.*, **96**, 7005 (1992)

207. J. K. Shin, J. Y. Yu and M. S. Jhon, Acceleration of Convergence Rates by High Directional Monte Carlo Sampling Procedure, *J. Chem. Phys.*, **97**, 9283(1992)

208. K. T. No, K. H. Cho, M. S. Jhon and H. A. Scheraga, An Empirical Method to Calculate Average Molecular Polarizabilities from the Dependence of Effective Atomic Polarizabilities on Net Atomic Charge, *J. Am. Chem. Soc.* , 115, 2005 (1993)

209. S. K. Kang and M. S. Jhon, On the Conformational Stability of Tactic p(HEMA) Hydrogels in Aqueous Solution, *J. Poly. Sci.* , 31, 1243 (1993)

210. S. K. Kang and M. S. Jhon, Ionic Mobility and Contact Ion Pairing Study by 23Na, 35Cl and 39K NMR in a Poly(methacrylic acid-co-N,N-dimethylamino)ethyl methacrylate) Hydrogel, *Macromolecules*, 26, 171 (1993)

211. H. G. Kim, J. H. Lee, H. B. Lee and M. S. Jhon, Dissociation Behavior of Surface-Grafted Poly(Acrylic Acid); Effects of Surface Density and Counterion Size, *J. Colloid Interface Sci.* , 157, 82 (1993)

212. J. D. Song and M. S. Jhon, Interaction between Na+ and Polymer in Aqueous Solutions of Na Salts of Poly(HEMA-Co-MAANa) studied by 23Na NMR, *J. Poly. Sci.* ,**31**,1687(1993)

213. M. S. Jhon and J. K. Shin, Prediction of the Global Energy minimum Conformation of Polypeptides by HDMC Procedure, *Supramolecular Chemistry*, 1, 139 (1993)

214. N. S. Kang, J. K. Shin, J. H. Yoon and M. S. Jhon, MD Study on the Electrostatic Effect of Protein Conformation, *J. Molec. Struc.* , **295**,185 (1993)

215. J. M. Park, K. T. No, M. S. Jhon and H. A. Scheraga, Determination of Net Atomic Charges Using a Modified Partial Equalization of Orbital Electronegativity Method, 3. Application to Halogenated and Aromatic Molecules. , *J. Comp. Chem.* , **14**, 1482 (1993)

216. J. Chang, H. D. Kim, T. Ree and M. S. Jhon, The Conformational Effects of Form('!) Helical poly(L-proline) and Form(a!) Helical poly(L-proline) to the Complex Formation with Helical poly(L-glutamic acid) through H-Bonding, *J. Poly Chem.* , 31, 3377 (1993)

217. J. H. Yoon and M. S. Jhon, MD Studies of Ca2+ Binding Effect on Calmodulin, *J. Molec. Struc.* , **295**, 193 (1993)

218. J. W. Lee, F. H. Ree and M. S. Jhon, Thermodynamic Perturbation Theory of Charged Hard Spheres in a Uniform Neutralizing Background, *Chem. Phys.* , **178**, 105 (1993)

219. G. Y. Kweon and M. S. Jhon, Distribution of H-bonded Rings in Pure Liquid Water & CH4 Solution by MC Method, *J. Molec. Liq.* , **59**, 195 (1994).

220. K. T. No, K. H. Cho, M. S. Jhon and H. A. Scheraga, Determination of the Proton Transfer Energies and the Lattice Energies of Several Amino Acid Zwitterions, *J. Phys. Chem.* , **98,** 10742 (1994).

221. O. S. Choi, S. H. Yuk, H. B. Lee and M. S. Jhon, Electric-Field-Sensitive Polymers ; Reversible Bendings of Rod-Shaped Polymer Gels in Salt Solutions, *J. Appl. Poly. Chem.* , **51**, 375 (1994)

222. J. U. Yu, J. K. Shin and M. S. Jhon, The Structure of Water in Human *ras* Oncogene Proteins, *Int. J. Quantum Chem.* . , **51**, 241 (1994)

223. J. K. Jung, M. S. Jhon and F. H. Ree, Homo and Hetero Coordination in Nonadditive Hard Sphere Mixtures and a Test of the van der Waals One Fluid Model, *J. Chem. Phys.* , **100**, 528 (1994)

224. J. K. Jung, M. S. Jhon and F. H. Ree, An Analytic Equation of State and Structural Properties of Nonadditive Hard Sphere Mixtures, *J. Chem. Phys.* , **100**, 9064 (1994)

225. T. K. Kim, M. Y. Song and M. S. Jhon, Theoretical Study on the Water Structure of the Aqueous Amino acid Solutions Using the Monte Carlo Method, *J. Molec. Liq.* , **59**, 179 (1994).

226. S. K. Kang, J. H. Yang, Y. K. Sung and M. S. Jhon, The Correlation between the Swelling Transition and the Hydrophobiaty on Tactic Poly(2-hydroxyethyl methacrylate) Hydrogels Surface in Aqueous Urea Solutions, *J. Colloid. Interface Sci.* , **167,** 371 (1994)

227. S. H. Choi, J. Y. Yu, J. K. Shin and M. S. Jhon, MD Simulations of trans- and cis-N-Acethyl-N'-Methylamides of Xaa-pro Dipeptides, *J. Molec. Struc.* , **323,** 233 (1994).

228. J. H. Yang and M. S. Jhon, The Conformation and Dynamic Study of Amphoteric Copolymers, P(NaMES-co-METMA1) using Viscometry, 14N and 13Na NMR, *J. Poly. Sci.* , **33,** 2613 (1995)

229. H. G. Kim and M. S. Jhon, Temperature Dependence of Interaction between Water and Sodium Polymethacrylate in Water-Methanol Mixture, *J. Poly. Chem.* , **33,** 63 (1995)

230. T. K. Kim, J. H. Yoon, J. K. Shin and M. S. Jhon, Use of the HDMC Method to Predict the Low Energy Structures of Melitin, *Molec. Simulation.* , **15,** 177 (1995).

231. J. H. Yoon, J. K. Shin and M. S. Jhon, Determination of C-terminal Structure of Human C-Ha-Ras Oncogenic Protein, *J. Comp. Chem.* , **16,** 478 (1995).

232. J. W. Lee, R. Ryoo, M. S. Jhon and K. I. Cho, Bond Density and Physicochemical Properties of a Hydrogenated Silicon Nitride Film, *J. Phys. & Chem. Solids*, **56,** 293 (1995).

233. J. K. Jung, M. S. Jhon and F. H. Lee, Fluid-fluid Phase Separations in Nonadditive Hard Sphere Mixtures, *J. Chem. Phys.* , **102,** 1349 (1995)

234. J. Y. Yu, N. S. Kang and M. S. Jhon, Pressure and Temperature Dependence Study of the Denaturation of Ribonuclease A Solution, *Molecular Simulations,* **15,** 265 (1995).

235. K. T. No, O. Y. Kwon, S. Y. Kim, K. H. Cho, C. N. Yoon, Y. K. Kang, K. D. Gibson, M. S. Jhon and H. A. Scheraga, Determination of Non Bonding Potential Parameters for Peptides, *J. Phys. Chem.* , **99,** 13019 (1995)

236. J. M. Park, O. Y. Kwon, K. T. No, M. S. Jhon and H. A. Scheraga, Determination of Net Atomic Charges Using a Modified Partial Equalization of Orbital Electronegativity Method. 4. Application to Hypervalent Sulfur- and

Phosphorous-Containing Molecules, *J. Compt. Chem.* , **16,** 1011 (1995)

237. K. T. No, O. Y. Kwon, S. Y. Kim, M. S. Jhon and H. A. Scheraga, A Simple Functional Representation of Angular-Dependent Hydrogen-Bonded Systems. 1. Amide, Carboxylic Acid, and Amide-Carboxylic Acid Pairs, *J. Phys. Chem.* , **99,** 3478 (1995).

238. V. P. Voloshin, Y. I. Naberukhin, N. N. Medvedev and M. S. Jhon, Investigation of Free Volume Percolation under the Liquid-Glass Phase Transition, *J. Chem. Phys.* , **102,** 4981 (1995)

239. N. S. Kang, J. Y. Yu and M. S. Jhon, The Effect of Cosolvent on a Tripeptide Solution Using MD Simulation, *J. Molec. Structure,* **355,** 201 (1995).

240. V. P. Voloshin, Y. I. Naberukhin, N. N. Medvedev and M. S. Jhon, On Percolation Character of the Liquid Glass Phase Transition, *Zh. Struct. Khim,* **36,** 473 (1995).

241. J. W. Lee, S. H. Lee, H. J. Yoo, M. S. Jhon and R. Ryoo, Annealing Effects in the Hydrogenated SiN Films during High Energy Ion Beam Irradiation, *J. Electrochem. Soc.* , **142,** 3210 (1995).

242. M. S. Jhon and J. Chang, Polypeptide-Polypeptide Complexes, *The Polymeric Materials Encyclopedia,* CRC Press, N. Y. (1996)

243. E. S. Kim, N. S. Kang and M. S. Jhon, MD Studies on the Effect of TFP in Ca2+ Binding Process of Calmodulin, *J. Molec. Struc.* , **380,** 101 (1996)

244. J. C. Jung, K. K. Lee and M. S. Jhon, The Dispersion of Polymethylsilsequinoxane into Polyimide, *Polymer Bulletin,* **36,** 67 (1996)

245. S. R. Kim, K. H. Lee and M. S. Jhon, The Effect of ZnCl2 on Polysulfone Solution, *J. Mem. Sci.* , **119,** 59 (1996)

246. Y. Kwong, S. Y. Kim, K. T. No, Y. K. Kang, M. S. Jhon and H. A. Scheraga, Determination of Potential Parameters for Amino Acid Zwitterions, *J. Phys. Chem.* , **100,** 17160 (1996)

247. K. T. No, B. H. Chang, S. Y. Kim, M. S. Jhon and H. A. Scheraga, Description of the Potential Energy Surface of Water Dimer with Artificial Neural Network, *Chem. Phys. Lett.* , **271**, 152 (1997)

248. D. H. Jung, N. S. Kang and M. S. Jhon, Site-Directed Mutation Study on Hyperthermostability of Rubredoxin from Pyrococous Furiosus Using M. D. Simulations in Solution, *J. Phys. Chem. A.* , **101**, 466 (1997)

249. S. R. Kim, S. H. Yuk and M. S. Jhon, A Semi-Interpenerating Network System for a Polymer Membrane, *Eur. J. Polymer,* **33**, 1009 (1997)

250. S. D. Hong and M. S. Jhon, Restricted Random Search Method Based on Taboo Search in the Multiple Minima Problem, *Chem. Phys. Lett.* , **267**, 422 (1997)

251. S. H. Cho, M. S. Jhon, S. H. Yuk and H. B. Lee, Temperature-Induced Phase Transition of Poly(N. N-dimethylaminoethylmethacrylate-co-acrylamide), *J. Poly. Phys.* , **595** (1997)

252. S. D. Hong and M. S. Jhon, Calculation of Excess Free Energy from the Averaged Effective Acceptance Ratio for the Lennard-Jones Fluid and the Inverse Twelve Fluid, *Chem. Phys. Lett.* , **273**, 79 (1997)

253. Y. K. Sung, M. -S. Son, and M. S. Jhon, Exohedral and Endohedral Complexation Energies of Complexes of $X@C70$ between Higher Fullerene and Rare-Gas Atoms(X = He, Ne, Ar, Kr, Xe), *Inorganica Chimica Acta,* **272**, 33 (1998)

254. J. S. Hong, D. H. Jung and M. S. Jhon, MD Study on Winter Flounder Antifreeze Protein and its Binding Mechanism, *Molec. Simulation,* **20,** 303 (1998)

255. K. K. Lee, J. C. Jung and M. S. Jhon, Maleic Anhydride Type ArF Photoresist, *Polymer Communications*, **39**, 4457(1998)

256. B. C. Shin, M. S. Jhon, H. B. Lee and S. H. Yuk, Temperature-Induced Phase Transition of Semi-Interpenetrating Polymer Network Composed of PNIPAM and Hydrophilic Polymers, Eur. Polym. J. , **34**, 171 (1998)

257. S. H. Yuk, S. H. Cho and M. S. Jhon, Temperature-Sensitive Polymer System Contrasted with Sodium Alginate and Poly DMAEMA-coAAM, *ACS Symposia Series,* **728**, 14 (1998)

258. B. C. Shin, M. S. Jhon, H. B. Lee and S. H. Yuk, pH/Temperature Dependent Phase Transition of an Interpenetrating Polymer Network Anomalous Swelling Behavior above LCST, *Eur. Polym. J.* , **34**, 1675 (1998)

259. S. H. Choi and M. S. Jhon, Valley Restrained Monte Carlo Procedure as a Method to Improve Sampling Efficiency, *Molecular Simulation*, **22**, 123 (1999)

260. S. H. Cho, M. S. Jhon and S. H. Yuk, Temperature-Sensitive Swelling Behavior of Polymer Gel Composed of Poly(N,N-Dimethylaminoethyl Methacrylate) and its Copolymers, *Eur. Polym. J.* , **35**, 1841 (1999)

261. S. Y. Park, J. H. Yang, S. H. Yuk and M. S. Jhon, Temperature-Induced Phase Transition of Poly(N-n-propylacrylamide-co-butyl methacrylate-co-N,N-diethylaminoethyl methacrylate, *J. Poly. Phys.* , **37**, 1407 (1999)

262. D. H. Jung, J. H. Yang, and M. S. Jhon, The Effect of an External Field in the Sttrcture of Water Using MD Simulations, *Chem. Phys.* , **244**, 331 (1999)

263. S. H. Choi, S. O. Hong and M. S. Jhon, Taboo-based M C Search as a Method to improve sampling efficiency, *Molec. Simulation*, **23**, 151 (1999)

264. C. C. Chai and M. S. Jhon, MD Study on Protein and its Water Structure at High Pressure, *Molec. Simulation* **23**, 257 (2000)

265. C. C. Choi, S. H. Choi, and M. S. Jhon, A Modified Valley Restricted M. C. Method to Efficiently search the Low Energy Structures of Peptides, *Molec. Simulations*, **25**, 385 (2000)

266. K. W. Jang, S. H. choi, S. I. Pyun and M. S. Jhon, The Effect of Water Content, Acidity, Temperature and Alcohol Content of the Acidic Sol-Gel Polymerization of TEUS with MC Simulations, *Molec. Simulations*, **27**,1 (2001)

267. S. Y. Park, S. H. Cho, S. H. Yuk and M. S. Jhon Characterization of Temperature-Induced Phase Transition of Polymer Complex Composed of Poly DMAEMA and Poly EAAm. by 'H NMR Relaxation Time Measurement, *European Polymer J.* , **37**,179 (2001)

268. N. S. Kang, D. H. Jung, K. T. No and M. S. Jhon, MD Simulation of Na^+ - DMP- and Na^+ - MP^{-2} Ion Pairs in Aqueous Solution, *Chem. Phys. Lett.* , 364, 580 (2002)

269 Y. I. Jhon, H. G. Kim and M. S. Jhon, The Structure of Water Near Pt and its Significance in Water-adsorbent Systems; MD Study, *J. Colloid and Interface Sci.* **260**, 9 (2003)

270 K. W. Jang, S. I. Pyun and M. S. Jhon, The Role of Excess Water in Acidic Sol-Gel Polymerization of TEOS Using MD Simulation, *Molec. Simulation,* **29**, 489 (2003)

271 N. S. Kang, K. T. No and M. S. Jhon, A Study on the H-bonded Network Around the Left-handed and Right-handed DNA in Ionic Solution, *Molec. Simulation,* **29**, 83 (2003)

272 Y. I. John, H. G Kim and M. S. Jhon, Equilibrium Between Two Liquid Structures in Water; Explicit Representation via Significant Liquid Structure Theory, *J. Molec Liq.* , in press (2004)